Poppycock!

Poppycock!

A Curmudgeon's Look at the
Myths That Keep Writers
from Writing

By
Geoff Hoff

All rights reserved. No part of this book may be reproduced mechanically, electronically, or by any other means, including photocopying, without written permission of the publisher. It is illegal to copy this book, post it to a website, or distribute it by any other means without express permission from the publisher.

Portions of this book have appeared in different form on several of my blogs and in the book The Inner Game of Internet Marketing.

Copyright © 2014 by Geoff Hoff
Paperback ISBN: 978-1-937988-16-6
Kindle ISBN: 978-1-937988-17-3

Hunter's Moon Publishing
http://HuntersMoonPublishing.com

Author cover photo by Kurt Scholle

Table of Contents

Introduction.. *vii*

Part One - The Myths We Hold Dear

    1 Why We Stop Ourselves.. 3

    2 The Myth of Inspiration 9

    3 The Myth of Talent... 19

    4 The Myth of Rules.. 25

    5 The Myth of Writer's Block... 29

    6 The Myth of "Write What You Know"........................... 33

    7 The Myths of Clichés, Ego and Purple Prose 35

    8 Hope, the Enemy of Art.. 43

    9 The Myth of Perfection... 51

Part Two - What to Do About Them

    10 The Power of Possibility 61

    11 Write. Right? 69

    12 Putting Off Procrastination... 75

    13 Getting Started 85

    14 Criticism and Praise 89

Part Three - The Nitty-Gritty

15 How to Rite Gud 95
16 The Structure of Writing 101
17 Writing Fiction 107
18 Some Writer's Exercises 115
19 And So It Goes 125

Resources 129
About the Author 131

Introduction

If you're a writer, write. Don't let anything stop you. Don't let anything get in your way. If you're a painter, paint. A sculptor? Sculpt. If you're a ditch digger, dig the damn ditch. If you are a musician, music, for goodness sake.

Got that? Okay.

You don't have to read this book, now, that's basically all I'm saying on every page.

Okay, so read the book. You will learn stuff. You will disagree with me. I may make you angry or make you laugh, or maybe even make you think, but the point is, if you call yourself a creative artist, create art. That's all you need do. Everything else is just an excuse and we creative types have enough excuses not to create that we don't have to buy in to any more. I almost wrote "don't have to create more excuses", but that would really make the whole notion of creativity kind of moot, wouldn't it?

Nothing I tell you is important except when I tell you to write. Write every day. Create every day if you aren't a writer. Nothing else matters. You already know that, but hearing it

Poppycock!

from someone you consider an "expert", for some reason, makes it more real so you are more willing to do it. If that's the case for you, I don't mind you considering me an expert. As long as that helps you sit your damn butt down and getting to work. If it doesn't help do that, don't you dare think of me as an expert. It's a meaningless accolade and I don't accept it.

So. You see that I can be a bit of a curmudgeon. This is something I have spend years developing. I have long been the nice guy who wants and is mostly able to please anyone and everyone. However, I like the sound of the word curmudgeon, so I set my goal to become one. What you hold in your hand is proof that I succeeded.

Read the book. Then get to work.

Geoff Hoff
November 2014

Part One

The Myths We Hold Dear

1
Why We Stop Ourselves

We artists are an interesting bunch. We think of ourselves as delicate, fragile, and, somehow, special. We are also, often, plagued by the notion that we aren't really up to snuff, which often conflicts with our over-inflated sense of talent and worth in a boisterous conflagration of feelings that will stop us short every time the notion that we might want to create something rears its little head. We also, often, have the vague feeling that the creative act requires hard work and, because this is a vague, therefore almost completely unexamined, notion, we fall back into our chaise lounge with the back of our hand on our brow and succumb to a case of the vapors. Or, for the more Papa Hemmingway among us, we drink.

I have been known to, when the thought of starting a new project or continue on an existing one crosses my mind, suddenly realize that the dishes need doing, or that I haven't mopped the living room floor for, probably, six years and now would be a grand time to do it. I get more laundry done when in the throes of a creative idea than at any other time in my life, and heaven help me if I discover, during one of these times, that I am out of (or even almost out of) ketchup (it doesn't matter if I haven't planned on cooking a hamburger anytime soon, it's the principle!) or bread or curry powder. A trip to the store becomes an absolute necessary. And, if it's a nice day, that trip should be on foot or by bicycle because, heaven knows, I don't get nearly enough exercise.

We have enough of a natural tendency to just not get stuff done that we don't really need to find new excuses for shirking our duty to the muse and the world. Oh, but we do find new excuses. And when we can't find them, we create them, or we listen intently to the conversations of others to see if there is a new kind of excuse for running around that we haven't yet had the pleasure of using.

Notice that I started out describing a myth. The myth that creating art is hard work. This whole section has been an examination of how that myth plays out in our lives.

Myths

Myths that artists carry around, when unacknowledged, can thwart their creativity. Let's look more deeply at myth itself. Myths are important to the development and cohesion of a society, and often art is where the myths are codified and perpetuated.

The early Greek plays were often almost religious ceremonies, where the mythos of the people was presented in an exciting way. Most, if not all, art during the early days of Christianity was for the purpose of expressing Christian stories, philosophy, iconography and ideology. This was true through the "age of enlightenment", which started in the 1500's with the alchemists and went into the late 1700's. Even during that time, "enlightenment" or "reason", which were the buzz words of the age (if you'd allow me to use a dreadful anachronism) were couched in terms that agreed with, or at least didn't greatly break from, religious thought.

Joseph Campbell talked long and interestingly about the "Hero's Journey" and how it relates to modern Western society, and he said it much better than I could hope to, but here I'll make an attempt to add to that discussion.

The hero's journey in Western myth, as described and defined by many people who have studied it, (briefly and condensed) starts with the hero having an opportunity that makes a change in his life, creates an entirely new situation. There is then a change of plans, or a second turning point. He reaches a point where he can no longer go back (the point of no return), then a major setback, after which he gives his final effort, leading to the climax, then resolution. This "formula" is an interesting thing to take into your writing.

I don't in any way advocate forcing your story to meet these story points. The reason for presenting them is that, we in the West are already attuned to this journey subconsciously, because our stories and myths, the ones we hold inside, the ones we learned to interact with others with, the ones we subconsciously live our life through, have followed a version of this timeline. It has become ingrained in our thought process. If this is so, it would serve the artist to tap in to this structure in order to talk directly to the readers' innards.

A great example of where this was used very, very consciously was in the movie Star Wars. George Lucas studied Joseph Campbell and very purposefully and directly used his ideas of the hero's journey in the script of his movie. Whether or not you personally like Star Wars, you must admit that it entered into the national consciousness very, very quickly and has continued to live there for many years. Even given the horrible second trilogy that threatened to dethrone the original three! Just my opinion.

(I am not one to espouse a formula in your writing or creation of art. I love experimentation and risk in art.) This is an example of how we can effectively use the myths that are already part of who we are. Now, in keeping with the Star Wars analogy, let's enter the dark side.

I have recently been accused of being reactionary. The person didn't mean that I espouse ultra conservative political views, or that I want desperately to return to an older time. They meant that much of my writings on the process of writing have been reactions to things others say rather than new things I say or new thoughts I may have. There is some truth to this. I often react strongly to what have become rules in any art form. (See the chapter on Rules if you want that in full screed mode.) It is how I examine them for myself.

I think rules are important. I think you need to know the ins and outs of your particular discipline. However, I think you also need to know that they are myths perpetrated by the agreement of a society over many years. Myths are important, but they aren't true.

We often equate the word "Myth" with something that isn't valid. "Oh, that's a myth. In actuality…" etc. (Well, most of us wouldn't say "actuality", but I'm pretentious and verbose. Go with me or move along.) We think of myths as quaint beliefs from an older time. Things like Mount Olympus and unicorns. Remember, these things weren't considered myths by the people who lived believing in them. They were only called myths once a "more enlightened" people from later times examined them. What will future generations consider myths that we now hold as truth?

Myths are valid. Society needs myths in order to function. Any discipline needs myths in order to perpetuate itself. However, when we equate "myth" with "truth" we can get trapped into a difficult corner.

Myths have power over us when they are unacknowledged. When they haven't been examined and understood in context. Once they are examined, we can choose to follow them or consciously circumvent them. At a more basic level, every individual has his own myths. One of mine might be that we need to rename our "truths" as "myths" so we can examine them. I have examined that myth and choose to still live within its precepts.

The myths that I am examining in this book, the myth of inspiration, the myth of writer's block and "write what you know", etc., all came about because they were useful to the writer, to the artist. They helped the artist produce. When adhered to as if they were immutable universal law, however, they control our process in an unproductive way.

I will continue to examine (and, sometimes, debunk) what I see as myths in the writing process. In that process, I may unwittingly create my own myths that need to be examined. That's how it works.

2
The Myth of Inspiration

Let's start with a biggie. I use the word "inspiration" a lot, but when I use it, I usually mean it in terms of wanting to achieve a greater good or aspire to a greater goal because of something or someone I have encountered along the way. Let's use Nelson Mandela as an example. What he was able to do, to accomplish, despite the circumstances in his life (or perhaps because of those circumstances) proves what humans are capable of, given the proper amount of passion and commitment. He inspires me. How about Bono. What he has done with his fame and money, the good he has achieved, the minds, bodies, societies he has affected in positive ways proves that money and power can be used for good. That inspires me. The ocean inspires me. It is a grand and powerful example of the miracle of creation and the small, important place we have within that.

I am inspired by spontaneous expressions of affection, by anonymous acts of charity, by conspicuous acknowledgment of good work and good deeds. I am inspired by those who come to see their potential, and those who strive to fulfill it with dedication. I am inspired by much in my life. Even, sometimes, chocolate cake, if it is dark and rich enough.

Writers, artists in general, use the word "inspiration" with a different meaning. We think of it as some sort of divine spark, the kiss of the Muse, some still, small voice whispering eloquent ideas that bypass all our mental faculties and allow us to create spontaneously. Many even wait around for this inspiration to hit, all the while producing nothing, affecting no one.

I think, for the most part, that inspiration thought of in this way is a myth.

I can hear the hoots from artists everywhere. My own inner artist is hooting right now, as I type. I'm sure I will get people wanting to express to me in the most vehement terms the almost out-of-body experiences they have had when deep in the creative process. Yes. I know. I have experienced those wonderful moments, also. Or rather, not moments, they seem outside of time. When in that kind of creative state, time no longer exists for you, nor do the needs of your body. Or your family. Or that noisy cat who hasn't been fed for the fourteen hours you have been under the spell of it.

This is not really inspiration. Many artists use that notion to exclude the general populace from thinking they can create art. "It is something only we special people have." Pheh. Anyone can learn to have those experiences. It is not a Muse whispering new thoughts into your ears. It is not from outside yourself. It is, instead, the flower that grows in a well-tilled garden. Those thoughts, those creations, occur because you have cleared the way for them, sometimes over a very long period of time, often without you realizing that's what you are doing, but you can do it consciously.

I am often asked where I come up with ideas. The easy answer would be "I was inspired". It's one I rarely use, even when I'm being lazy. Which is most of the time, if confessions are the thrust of the day. The truth is that I have trained my mind to think, and when your mind thinks, it will come up with some surprising things. I observe all the time. But I observe in a way that many people don't. It's a simple adjustment that anyone can make, and I recommend making it: I have trained myself to notice my observations. Sometimes they then become dormant for years, bubbling and boiling in what Paul Sheele calls the "other than conscious mind." But if I hadn't noticed them consciously, they would remain external, unusable.

To go back to the image of the flowers in a well-tilled garden, a farmer can spend years clearing the land, pulling the rocks out, softening the soil, fertilizing it with good, old-fashioned cow dung. This is you being educated, you reading, you letting other art wash over you, letting the world wash over you consciously. The farmer plants the seeds early. Some bulbs get planted years before they bloom. It can take an acorn up to a half century to produce another acorn, but that does not mean that second acorn spontaneously appeared after being whispered to by a Muse.

After the allotted time, the plants then grow. Some of them surprise you with their beauty, their strangeness, their originality, they seem effortless, but you have worked hard for them.

Leaving that analogy behind before it twists itself into something unrecognizable and unusable, if you train your mind to write, it will write. Journal. Jot. Train your mind to observe. Notice and admire stray thoughts. Notice and admire stray happenings. Notice and admire the mundane. As you notice and celebrate life you will "attract" more life worth celebrating because that's what you've trained yourself to notice and it's always already around you.

The more you encourage yourself to do that, the more you will be able to produce your art. You can call it inspiration if you want to, you can call it a gift from the Muse or the Divine or the Universe, you can call it Fred if you're desperate, but know that it is precisely (to go back to my rickety metaphor and mix it a little) because you have tilled your mind that the Muse and the Divine and the Universe can chat with you.

In the back section of this book, I will give you some nifty exercises that will help you till this garden a bit, and also help you once it's time to harvest the lovely fruit.

Suck It Up

There may be some days when you just don't want to. You can finish that sentence in any number of ways: you just don't want to go to work, you just don't want to cook, to clean. You just don't want to visit your Aunt Tess who always bakes great cookies but smells like old olives and boiled beef.

And some days you just don't want to write.

There are times when you can honor that, as long as you don't make a habit of it, but usually, if you need to write every day because it's your job or you have a deadline or you've made a promise, you've got to suck it up (which is a particularly odd expression, if you ask me.) Just get the fingers moving. When you get through the "I don't wanna" the magic will happen. And often times, the resistance to writing is like the little crust on a puddle in winter. When you tap on it with the tip of your shoe, it shatters.

Often, when we don't feel like writing, we give ourselves the excuse that there's nothing to write about. Poppycock. There is always something to write about. Write about not wanting to write, if nothing else comes to mind, and if it fits into your assignment. The simple exercise of pushing through the resistance will train your belligerent psyche that it doesn't have much sway, so it might as well just go back to bed for the day and let you get on with it.

And know that not wanting to is part of the process. The artist in us can be perverse, sometimes, and act like a spoiled child. Don't be a slave to that child. Push through it. Do it kindly, without judgment, but do it.

The Myth of the Fragile Muse

In college, my major course of study was acting. The theatre department was run, at that small school, like a professional acting company, and we produced a minimum of five plays a year. Everyone in the department was expected to do every job in the theatre at least once, and everyone was expected to be in the plays, on the stage, in front of an audience. It was heaven, if you can imagine four years of 14 hour days being anything like heaven.

There were people on the campus who weren't part of the department but wanted to participate. Of course they were welcome, there was always a lot to do. The professors used to caution them, however, to be very careful and respectful of the actors during rehearsal and performance nights because creativity was so fragile and so easily shut down.

I believed that wholeheartedly and to my core. I believed it partly because it put the actors a bit on a pedestal, but mostly because it fostered the notion that creativity was somehow special and unique to a particular breed of person and that not anyone could access that power. The fragility of that was a very romantic notion, a very seductive one. If I can hold something this fragile, nurture it, care for it gently, grow it into a willowy, wisp-like entity that needed constant care, I am, indeed, a very rare and talented person deserving of special consideration and special treatment. Pampering, by God!

Balderdash. I wonder why anyone suffered my presence.

Because I believed it about acting, I translated it into my writing and was very, very careful of my "Muse". I never forced myself to write if I just didn't feel like it. I feared chasing her away if I did. I feared that the willowy, wisp-like entity would blow away like smoke on a breeze and I'd be left without my soul.

Then I found myself in a situation where I had to write, I had a commitment and a time limit. My writing partner Steve Mancini and I were writing for an on-going stage production and the scripts had to come out in a very specific time-frame. "I don't wanna" wouldn't work, we had to produce scripts. Without even thinking about it, we simply sat down and did it.

I found myself in more and more similar situations as the years went by and it caused me to reexamine this belief I took on so heartily in my heady youth. If I could force myself to sit down and create something, even something worthy of putting in front of an audience, no matter what mood I was in or what willful resistance I was experiencing, perhaps that elusive Muse wasn't so fragile after all. Or so elusive. Damn it. Another excuse torn asunder.

When you get into the habit of writing every day, your Muse will become robust. She will put her head high, puff out her ample bosom, put on boxing gloves and soundly knock any impediment to getting ideas into your grey matter out of her way, then dance around punching the inside of your head until you pay attention to her. The more you write, the more power and vitality she will have. Think Brunhilda with spear, shield and horned hat. Not someone who could be blown away by a mere breeze. Metaphor aside, the more you write, the more power and vitality you will have.

Yes, sometimes the best way to write is to push away from the keyboard and take a walk. This is sound advice for anyone who is creative. But there is a big difference between stepping away to let the juices flow and stepping away to indulge in a bit of "I don't wanna."

If you don't want to, and are afraid you'll damage your creative flow by forcing it, get over your little self, sit down and start typing. You're muse will thank you for it.

Having To

Having to write rather than wanting to write can be a marvelous thing. Having to write whether you want to or not. I'm not talking about some person shaking a finger at you and making you sit at your computer, I'm talking about the powerful obsession where every cell in your body screams out that you need to sit down and compose words, that anxiety that makes everything you do that isn't writing feel wrong. It is a magnificent compulsion and I am loath to deny it.

It isn't always like that for me and I have trained myself to produce even when I don't have that inner, throbbing drive, but I love when that drive kicks in. It often happens after I've had an idea for a new project and have done some of the background work for it. All those bits and pieces have been swirling around in my head and begin to coalesce into some alchemical gold.

I will be washing dishes or driving to the store and the story will suddenly insist on grabbing my attention and grabbing hard. When it happens at home, I run and start taking notes. When it happens on the road, I repeat the phrases I'm hearing in my brain over and over until I can get to a place to write them down. It is almost a completely automatic reaction that I don't consciously control.

I first noticed this obsession back in college when I was learning acting. I would begin a new role for a new production and would start the homework, the work imagining myself into the circumstances of the person I was to be. Those circumstances would take hold of me and I would obsessively think about them all the time. When I started writing more seriously, the same thing happened but with a slight difference. Whole passages of the piece I was working on would appear as if by magic. It has happened in that moment before sleep and I've trained myself to force myself out of bed to get it down. Even if it's really cold and I can't find my slippers. It takes a long time for the computer to boot up, so I go over and over the imagery until I can get my word processor open and get it down. If I don't do that, I'll either not be able to get to sleep or I will have forgotten it by morning.

Either option makes me grumpy, and we don't want that to happen.

When I don't act on these obsessive moments, either by committing them to memory so I can get them down or getting them down right away, the obsession fades and when the obsession fades, it becomes difficult to get back to work. Also, when it fades, I feel like the sun has moved a little further away.

Why do I write? Because I have to. Because I love to. Because I can't imagine not writing.

The Myth of Balance

We often hear that we must put balance into our lives. Some of us, it seems, work too much. Some of us, by some standards, play too much. Some spend too much time with friends, some, not enough or too much with family. Some are always alone, some always surrounded by noise and chaos. The idea, we are told, is to balance it all out so that we are living a full and satisfying life.

Well, I say Poppycock! That kind of balance is practically impossible to achieve, so worrying about it only causes stress and isn't helpful at all. That kind of balance makes me think of the word "average". There will be no peaks and no valleys. It has very little excitement and has very little room for creativity or inspiration.

When I am in the throes of creating something new, a product or course, a story or novel, a stage production, every waking moment is dedicated to it. Everything else is secondary. Sometimes, even eating and sleeping become intrusions. People who know and love me need to understand that it's what I do, how I function, and if I can't function that way, I can't function.

Yes, you must take care of your obligations. For much of my life, I worked at various full time jobs. I did them well and still managed to be obsessively dedicated to whatever project I was working on. If I'd had a family, I would have needed to make sure the bills were paid, the roof didn't leak and a hug and kiss were exchanged every now and then. However, I think the whole, relatively new notion of 24/7 "hands on" parenting does no one any good. The parents are frazzled to a crisp and the kids never get to experience creating their life for themselves, with all the mistakes and boo-boos that entails.

Most of us who grew up in the 50s, 60s and 70s had very little hands on parenting. I played with my brothers and sister in the fields behind my house and the brook across the street until we moved to the city, then I busied myself with paper routes and school activities that I got myself to. I got cuts and scrapes. They healed. I got into exactly one fight (one punch was thrown, not by me) and I survived. My mother never once drove me to a play or orchestra rehearsal. She did come to (most) of the shows I did, but she had a full-time, evening job through most of my junior high and high school years so I learned to manage.

Because of this, when I went to college, I was used to taking care of myself and didn't have the freshman year crazies trying to figure it all out. I have been responsible for myself my entire life. And I turned out relatively sane and productive.

If you want to create something of meaning on the planet, if you want to make a difference, which is what we all talked about in the naive and wistful 60s and 70s, you have to let things go decidedly unbalanced. Connie Ragen Green often says that, "If you do for a year what others won't, you can live for the rest of your life the way others can't." Stop striving for balance. Give yourself permission to be obsessed with what you're already obsessed with.

Only then can you create something revolutionary.

Don't Wait for Inspiration

I know a lot of writers (and painters and musicians and even people who have to write for their job!) who feel they have to wait to be inspired before they sit down to work. They wait for that "still, small voice" that will guide them to the keyboard (or easel or instrument) and make them produce their latest work of staggering genius.

Please. Don't wait to be inspired. First of all, if you are moving through life at a normal modern pace, if that small voice actually does speak to you, chances are you'll miss it or mistake it for indigestion. But, more seriously, when you sit down to write (or paint or... okay, you get the picture) the inspiration will naturally flow.

The more consistently you do it, the more in the habit you will be of expressing yourself, and the more in the habit you are of expressing yourself the more your subconscious will give you to express. It happens backwards from the way people expect it to. Inspiration doesn't have you produce, producing "inspires" inspiration.

Be in the habit of writing, every day, or as close to every day as you can, and those flashes of insight will have a vehicle and a way to get your notice. They will trust that you will listen to them and they will show up more and more often. Don't sit down to write something brilliant. Just sit down to write. The more you do, the more chance there is of something brilliant happening.

3
The Myth of Talent

I had a life-changing exchange with a teacher, once. We were talking about pursuing our passions, our art. About spending our lives doing something we loved. I stood up in class and asked a question that had been burning in my heart for years: "What if I'm just not talented?"

He looked at me for a brief moment, then asked me, "What if you're not?"

That stopped me. Not at all what I expected him to say. At first I got mad. How could he even suggest that? (I was young and logic didn't enter in to it.) Then, as I considered more, I realized that it didn't matter at all. And it hasn't mattered ever since.

I've seen people who were truly talented who did nothing with their talent. I've seen people who had very little talent, but a lot of drive, that sailed in their chosen profession. Over the few months after that conversation, I slowly removed that question from my mind. I did it by saying to myself that I had absolutely no talent, and that I was going to pursue art anyway. It eased a very heavy burden. A burden I'd been carrying for what seemed a very long time in my young life.

I have worked hard over the years. I've developed my eye, my ear, my sensibilities. I've listened to words and read words and put words together. I've experimented and discovered what worked, what was effective, what wasn't as effective. My love of words was more than enough to keep me moving forward and by moving forward, my love of words and their power and beauty grew. I have been told, by some who seem to know what they're talking about, that I'm a good writer. If that is true, it's not because I'm talented, or, if I am talented, not because I'm more so than anyone else might be. Talent has little or nothing to do with the ability to combine words in such a way that they evoke a response.

I can use words well because I dream and I follow where my dreams lead.

Face It, You're Not Good Enough

A close companion of the myth of talent is the myth of worth. Many writers and other artists are often confronted by that voice put into their heads by family, teachers and society in general that they aren't good enough. They aren't talented enough. They are fooling themselves to even try.

If we aren't yet fully conscious of these thoughts, they can run our lives, and thwart our art. When we do become conscious of them, we notice that they crop up at the most inopportune times. Perhaps just when we are about to finish (or start) a new project. Perhaps just when we are about to sell the new project or just before the possibility of a new success.

Often, when we are confronted by these thoughts, we try to ignore them, which makes them louder. Stuffing them will give them power. To deny them sets up a lie in your energy.

Trying to fix them (or trying to fix yourself, which is the same thing) will more often than not simply frustrate you. We are not fixable creatures. Also, trying to fix it will put a lot of focus on it, which will keep it present in our mind and therefore more real and more solid.

There is, however, a way to deal with these thoughts.

Agree with them.

You are not worthy. You are not talented.

So what.

No one is worthy or talented, so why should you think you're special? Write anyway. This will take the wind out of that particular conversation very quickly. When the thought comes up, when your mother's voice or your father's voice or the voice of that very special teacher speaks in your head, "you're just not good enough to do this" agree with it, thank it and keep writing.

It's going to be there anyway, so you might as well have fun with it. It takes a lot less energy to just say, "Yeah, you're right. So?" than to spend months and years visualizing worthiness, which can't really be visualized because it isn't a thing you can see or an emotion you can feel. Agree with it and move on; use the energy you used to use fighting it writing.

Your Gnome

Let's look at that another way. We all have gnomes that follow us around and pop up at the most inopportune time. Some of yours might be named "I'm Just Not Good Enough" but they might be "They Must Know Better Than Me" and "I'm Not Capable". A writer might have a gnome called "No One Would Care About What I Have to Say." One of mine is named "It's Not Going to Work." They are insistent little beasts. You think you've vanquished them only to find them sitting next to you on the couch, looking up at you with oh, so innocent little eyes.

When they show up, our first instinct is to either completely ignore them or slay them, quickly and soundly. However, history tells us that the little beasts refuse to be ignored for long and are not known to stay slain, so what must we do?

I say, first we must acknowledge them. That in itself will defuse much of their power. Then it might be productive to see where they've come from. Most of our gnomes are there because at one time they were protecting us from something. Who knows what at this point. Perhaps the hurt received from a misguided friend or an uncomprehending adult. Perhaps the slight from a bully. It's probably not important to know what, exactly, but once you see that they are only there for your good, you can look at them in a completely different way.

Rather than trying to slay them, you might consider looking after them, caring for them.

"I see you hiding there behind the television set," you might say. Bid them come sit next to you, hug them and tell them softly, "You have done a wonderful job of protecting me. Thank you so much. I am very grateful. I'm much stronger, now, and can protect myself, so you can go outside and play." Then kiss them on the forehead and let them go with an affectionate pat on the fanny.

Once you do that, your resistance to them will disappear and, as we have been told, that which we resist persists. Once your resistance to them is gone, their power over you will be gone also. The gnome may still be there, may still creep in when you least want to see them, but you will have already undone their special magic.

So look after your gnome!

Everyone is Creative

Yes, even you. If you think you aren't, it's only because someone convinced you that creativity wasn't practical, that you couldn't make a living with it and you believed that to the point where you actually believed you weren't creative. Whoever that was (even if it was you) had your best interest at heart. They also should be slapped.

Think of when you were a child. Every movement, every thought, was a creative act. It was how you learned about the world around you. We all played. We made whole cities out of wooden blocks and fought dragons or had grand tea parties. In the Western world, that was "taught" out of us and that's a shame, because, no matter what you do, if you add creativity to it, you'll do it better.

I can prove you are creative in about twenty seconds. Don't believe me? Try this:

Are you ready? Okay. I want you to sit down and think of a lemon. The skin is yellow, almost waxy smooth. It has a slightly bumpy texture when you run your finger across it.

Now imagine picking up a sharp knife cutting into that lemon. At first, the knife resists a little, then slices through easily. When you open the lemon, the inside is cool and moist. It emits a pleasant odor. Imagine that odor for a moment. It's tart and clean smelling.

Touch the inside with the tip of your finger. It's wet, but it's a smooth wetness. You can also feel the lemon pulp.

Now pick up one half of the lemon and raise it up to your mouth. Squeeze just one small drop of the juice onto your tongue. That cool, tart drop rolls to the back of your tongue.

Did you pucker? Did your mouth water, even a little?

Congratulations! You are now officially creative! And here's why. You took a lemon and visualized it. You touched it. You actually tasted it and it made your mouth water. But there isn't a lemon in site, so where is it?

Poppycock!

You created that lemon out of nothing. Out of your imagination. You created something out of nothing. You are creative. We've now put that worry to bed. What's next?

4
The Myth of Rules

I've already talked a little bit about rules, but let's delve. The whole point of this book, really, is that things people think of as writing rules often just get in the way of good writing. Are there any rules for writing that the writer should be aware of? Certainly. One such rule is, "don't use sentence fragments". An example of a sentence fragment, for those who missed the inherent irony, is "Certainly."

Proper use of grammar is important. Knowing when to use "he" and when to use "him", for instance: Is it "I went to the store with he and Irene" or "I went to the store with him and Phyllis." In this case, the easiest way to know which to use is to cut the "and" phrase from the sentence and see which one works. "I went to the store with he" is obviously wrong, so the second example is the correct one. (Unless you actually went to the store with her and Gregory, in which case the sale meat you purchased is probably tainted.)

However, there are times when you might do exactly that for effect. (A subtle effect, to be sure, as most in America would probably miss it.) One way to break it is in dialogue where, depending on the character talking, most grammar rules can simply be thrown out the window. Real people, when they talk, often don't know and therefore don't use, proper grammar. To make the dialogue true to the character, write as he or she would talk. (Him or her? No. He or she.)

You've heard not to start a sentence with "and" or "but". Many great writers do. You've heard that you shouldn't split an infinitive (put any word between "to" and the verb.) That rule only came into existence at the beginning of the 19th century because some priggish professors wanted English to sound more like Latin, which it never will, so to simply ignore that rule is to boldly go where good writers have gone before.

Knowing the rules of proper grammar is important and every writer should strive to learn them, if only because you can then break them much more effectively.

There is no "One Process"

So, "Is there one correct process to use to write?"
The short answer is, "No."
That's pretty short, and not very helpful, so I'll augment it a bit with a more complete answer.

I do have my process, honed over the years. It works for me, but, as with every individual writer's process, mine is uniquely my own, and, as with every individual writer's process, is a wonderful, delightful, sometimes harrowing mystery.

However, there are things I've discovered along the way that are useful to me and might be useful to any writer. To you, for instance. I have also heard (and tried) all the "rules" for writing that all the smart people espouse. Some of them, I have come to discover, are simply silly. Some of them are "clever" but not pragmatic. (I like to call those "bromides" not "rules".) Some sound great on first hearing them, but put into practical use are, frankly, useless. Some are wonderfully beneficial and I like to take those, use them, adjust them to my own quirks, then take full credit for them. (I kid. Sort of.)

What I present here is what I do, and, after several screenplays, a web-based comedy serial, a best-selling satirical novel, a popular web show, a long running, episodic stage show and several articles, opinion pieces, sales pages, blurbs, eulogies, books, short stories, press releases, forum postings and works of self adulation, it works fairly well for me. Any tips I present in this book are tips, not rules. Listen to them. Try them out. Adjust them to your own personality. Refute them and do something completely different then start your own writing tips book. As soon as you turn a suggestion or guideline into a rule, you have sapped its power. Or, more accurately, turned your own power over to that suggestion or guideline.

The real purpose of all this, though, isn't necessarily to tell you how to write, it is to tell you to write, and give hints that might help with that.

Why Most Advice to Writers Sucks

Many years ago, I had a subscription to Writer's Digest magazine. In almost every issue, there were articles such as:

"10 Writing Mistakes to Avoid"

"The 5 Top Reasons an Agent Will Reject Your Book"

"7 Query Don'ts"

"Why You Won't Sell Your Manuscript"

"The Top 10 Things You're Doing Wrong"

"Why You Suck as a Writer"

"100 Reasons to Just Give It All Up and Become an Accountant Like Your Mother Told You To"

Okay, so I'm exaggerating. A little. It got so that every time I opened the covers of the magazine, I felt more discouraged, until I almost quit writing. I canceled my subscription instead. Wise move.

(Full disclosure, I'm not saying don't read Writer's Digest. It has much in it that is useful and they gave Steve Mancini and me a marvelous commentary on our book Weeping Willow: Welcome to River Bend. You can find a link to that review at the end of the book, in the resource section.)

Much advice to writers is in the "what not to do" arena. I say, tell me what I can do. Inspire me to create. Creativity is a magical thing. Please, when you give advice, honor that magic. Open up possibilities for me. And especially, Don't Scare Me Away From Writing! Sheesh.

And if you are a writer, look for advisers who will do all that for you. They are out there. There are people who will excite you about what creativity can do, excite you about your own potential, who pull fetters off rather than strapping you in to them. Find people who open doors rather than telling you why the doors are closed. For goodness sake, find people who encourage you.

If you are creative, you are powerful and don't let anybody tell you otherwise. And we're all creative. See the chapter about talent.

5
The Myth of Writer's Block

    I suppose this is the myth that has caused more damage than any other to the writer's life, one of the biggest myths around. This is one that all creative people cling to earnestly and it is one of the biggest excuses people use to not write. Trust me, I know. I've used it myself on more than one occasion. It is the myth of writer's block. There are many strategies to overcome (or, more accurately, bypass) it. I'd first like to go more in depth about what writer's block really is.

    In the chapter on inspiration, I mentioned those who sit around waiting for inspiration to hit. This, I think, is what writer's block really is. When a writer is not in the habit of writing, either with a set schedule or a set number of pages, ideas won't flow, or won't automatically flow all the time. If ideas aren't flowing, the writer thinks there is nothing to write about. To hit a point I make often, all a writer is is one who writes. If the ideas aren't flowing, prime the pump by writing something. Anything. Type, "I have nothing to write" a hundred times. Your brain will come up with something, believe me. If only to get you to stop typing that. It might also slap you upside the head, so be careful.

More practically, describe in detail some object or person in your immediate environment. The dusty keyboard. The wilted plant. The stinky old cat. The stinky old roommate. Use as many of the senses as possible to viscerally evoke an experience with your words.

Again, when you do this, the pump will be primed.

Another aspect of writer's block is that a lot of writers, a lot of artists, feel that every time they sit down to create, what comes out must be brilliant with a capital "B" and a sparkly font. Give that thought up immediately! It is death to art. It won't allow you to test things or experiment. It won't allow you to write a long string of nonsense just to get the fingers moving and the mind engaged. It has happened to me that I wrote nothing but nonsense for days on end, but two thing happened because I did that:

1. It started to flow in a way that was almost hard to capture and
2. In looking back on the pages of nonsense, I discovered the kernel of many very cool ideas. I once wrote an entire short story based on a stray thought in my rambling pages. It was a very good short story. Once I opened up to the thought, the story came forth almost fully formed because I'd been cogitating on it the whole time I'd been writing the nonsense pages.

I rarely feel the need, anymore, to write nonsense pages, (when I feel what we call writer's block coming on, you can bet I do sit down and write nonsense.) I am in the habit of writing. It isn't that hard a habit to have. Nothing is stopping you. There is no such thing as writer's block. There is just "not writing" which can be handled very easily by writing. Yes, I'm repeating myself.

The Habit of Writing

A friend pointed me in the direction of a lovely quote that fits in perfectly with my notion of creativity. "Creativity is not a gift. It's a habit." I liked it so much I decided to look it up. It is from Twyla Tharp. In her book The Creative Habit, she said, "Creativity is not a gift from the gods bestowed by some divine and mystical spark." (Notice how close that is to what I have written about the myth of inspiration. It seems I have a compatriot in Ms. Tharp.) The book goes on to prove that creativity is the product of effort and within the reach of everyone who wants to achieve it, that in order to be creative you must simply be willing to make it a habit.

The habit of creativity is not difficult to cultivate. It is about training yourself to see, training yourself to listen and feel. There are people, of course, who have a natural facility for it just as there are those with a natural facility for movement or for eloquent speech, but anyone can develop it by spending a few moments every day simply observing, then observing their own observations. Creative leaps, those moments when something absolutely new seems to appear from out of nowhere, when a connection is suddenly made between two disparate things, are actually well prepared for even if that preparation is sub- or unconscious. Making it a conscious process gives you control over it, responsibility for it.

There are many who would not want the responsibility for their own creativity, but even that can be circumvented by engendering a habit of making things. Making anything. And doing it regularly.

Specifically for a writer, that habit can be developed by writing. Not by writing anything worthwhile or writing anything necessarily powerful or brilliant, but by writing. Writing anything and doing it regularly. Observe, then write what you have observed. Experience, then write what you have experienced. Contemplate, then write what you have contemplated. Do things, then write about what you have done.

Creativity is not a gift from the gods. It is not a divine spark. When it becomes a habit, it just seems that way.

6
The Myth of "Write What You Know"

We as writers have often heard the dictum or rule to "write what you know." I first heard this when in grade school, and it really puzzled me. I liked to read fantasy stories and wondered how they were written if that rule were true. When I heard it, I had just read Mary Mapes Dodge's Hans Brinker, or The Silver Skates about a young Dutch boy in Holland. It said in the forward that Ms. Dodge had never visited Holland, (she finally did after the book was published) and yet she evoked an experience or reality that was wonderful for a young reader.

I call it a myth, here, but only sort of. If you take the notion at face value, as many writing students have done, it will stifle your creativity. Had Jules Verne heard it and taken it to heart, we would be a much less rich society. If Arthur C. Clarke had done so, we would not have the communications satellite, which he envisioned in 1945. I'm sure J. R. R. Tolkien never actually visited Middle Earth.

However, if you dig more deeply, the dictum has truth and power. Ms. Dodge didn't know Holland first hand, but had:

    Done lots of research and

    Imagined herself into its environs

Because of this research and daydreaming, she did know the land, and know it well. This is also what Mr. Tolkien had done. He spent years imagining all the lands in Middle Earth, imagining their populations and creatures. He dreamed about them and knew them first hand. I'm sure Bilbo Baggins "spoke" to him, as many characters seem to do to the writers creating them, because Mr. Tolkien imagined him so completely that in his mind the Hobbit had become quite real. Tolkien, then, like Ms. Dodge, did ultimately write what he knew.

We also have the Internet, which writers of past generations didn't, to do the research. Then we can daydream about the facts to make them viscerally real in our experience. And daydreaming is fun. You can tell your spouse you're working if they ask why you're sitting on the couch with that silly blank expression on your face.

I think the originator of the rule had the best of intentions. If you feel stuck, write about what's in front of you. That is good advice. It's one of the exercises I recommend often. But when it was presented to me, it was communicated to mean "if you try to write about stuff you haven't experienced, it will be phony, which is bad."

Thank God I never listened!

7
The Myths of Clichés, Ego and Purple Prose

Avoid Clichés – Unless You Don't

I once had a thought that I hoped wouldn't become a cliché. It turned out that the thought was so cumbersome and convoluted that chances of that happening were very small. (I almost said moot, but that would be entirely too cliché.) However, it started my mind swirling around with the whole notion of cliché. It is almost a cliché to say, "avoid clichés at all cost." Actually, it's almost a cliché to say, "it's almost a cliché", so it's hard to avoid them. They are insidious, sneaky little buggers, and creep in to your writing without any warning.

Things that have become clichés usually started out as profound or poetic thoughts, very clever and original ways to either describe something familiar or make understandable something very obscure, but devolved due to over use to become almost meaningless. Salvador Dalí said of clichés,

"The first man to compare the flabby cheeks of a young woman to a rose was obviously a poet; the first to repeat it was possibly an idiot."

When used consciously, clichés can actually enhance good writing, they can be a comfortable entry point to a more complex bit of thought. They can be a good source of humor, especially if you somehow acknowledge that you realize you're using the cliché. If you're using several clichés strung together like pearls on a string, the turns of phrase can play well with others or fight like cats and dogs, they can gum up the works, or be your trump card, which can put the lie to thinking outside the box or become an actual Deus ex machina, making you eat your own words with an evil laugh, which is food for thought for anyone who sees the writing on the wall and really, really wants to avoid cliché. They also taste like chicken.

Okay, I think I just wrenched the soft tissue in my brain.

More seriously, as a writer of fiction, I always strive to avoid cliché phrases and (to use a cliché) turns of phrase. When I notice them on my page I try to reword them in a new and original way. "He breathed a sigh of relief" might become "He breathed in sharply, then released the breath slowly as he realized the shadow crossing his path was simply the old man who sold newspapers on the corner."

Doing this does two things. It makes your writing have more of a unique voice, and it will usually make it more viscerally exciting because you've had to experience, then describe what the cliché actually means, and that's what you really want to communicate to your reader.

Allow the clichés to be there in your first pass. Then, when you go back through to polish it, think about them. Make them yours. Wrestle them to the ground. To coin a phrase.

Big Words and Purple Prose

I am often accused of using too many big words when I write. Often the accusation is continued with "when a small one will do." I have several problems with that accusation. First of all, I don't use big words for the sake of using big words. (Yes, there may be a small element of showing off. I'm an artist. It's what we do.) I love words and believe they are there to be used. Words have shades of meaning, and the "big" word I use is chosen with those shades in mind. To say I should have used the word "small" instead of "infinitesimal" would be akin to telling an artist he should have used purple instead of that dusty blue-grey shade of mauve he used. It may not make the painting awful, but it would certainly change the character and feel of it.

It would be like telling Mozart he uses too many notes, as the Emperor did in the play Amadeus.

Besides the shades of meaning one word will have over another word, there are also the aesthetics of the word itself. I love the way they sound, the way they look on the page. Often, when attempting to describe a particular, specific event or situation, a word will occur to me that just sounds right, that will have a pleasing cadence to it, a soft blend of consonants as well as the soft blend of meanings. I will frequently look the word up (yea dictionary.com) to make sure it actually has the meaning or meanings I intend it to have. I am disappointed when I have I have misjudged the word somehow, and it means something else.

There are also times when I know there is exactly the right word and I can't find it in the jumble of imagery, clutter of facts and suppositions, and general disarray that calls itself my mind, when I'll pull out the thesaurus. (I use the Roget's Thesaurus, not those silly "dictionary-type" ones. Who thought those up? If you don't know how to use the thesaurus, learn.) I don't do this simply to find more big words to use, I'll often find a perfectly simple one I hadn't yet thought of. I do this because I know the right word is there and I want to use the right word.

I also get rather annoyed when writers and writing teachers talk about paring down word usage. Stephen King supposedly said "Any word you have to hunt for in a thesaurus is the wrong word." It's a coy and clever sentiment, Mr. King, but I respectfully disagree. As I just said, there have been many times when I knew the word I wanted, the one the passage needed, was there but couldn't find it in my chaotic brain. I often have those "Tip of the Tongue" words, and a thesaurus is a great way to flick them off the tongue and on to the page.

The Harbrace College Handbook, which is in its 13th edition, says that "The use of more words then necessary to express meaning is an offense to exact diction." I say to the estimable handbook, tell it to Shakespeare! Okay, you could argue that the meaning of "necessary" is the crux of the thing, and if it's necessary to use one hundred words where one will do, then fine, but people who say these things usually mean, "Use less words." I will use exactly the number of words I want to use to excite my ear, heart, mind and soul.

I like my purple prose. I like a well crafted, visceral (that lovely word again!) passage full of description that sings to me as I read it. It's fine for Raymond Carver, who is said to have prized brevity in writing and wrote some wonderful stories, to be terse in his writing. (And anyway, it was editor Gordon Lish that pared down Carver's words, not Carver.) Give me Christopher Fry who took three pages to say what might have been said in two Carverian words. And what pages they were! In his wonderfully dark and funny "A Phoenix Too Frequent", Mr. Fry has his young, naive heroine, while talking to her maid, Doto, rhapsodizing about her dead husband's qualities: "He was the ship. He had such a deck, Doto, such a white, scrubbed deck. Such a stern prow, such a proud stern, so slim from port to starboard. If ever you meet a man with such fine masts give your life to him, Doto." So much better than "he was like a boat."

Don't tell me to pare my words down. Don't tell me to "omit needless words" or that "vigorous writing is concise" as E.B. White does in Elements of Style. I'll just ignore you, anyway. Pare your own words down and leave mine alone. Okay, Mr. White does have a point, and is usually just taken out of context, but it is that context that I so react to when people tell me to simplify my writing.

The following is the opening of one of my short stories, called "Death of the Loch Ness Monster". In it, a woman observes her napping husband, someone she has become disenchanted with:

> She watched him sleeping in the middle of the living room; an overstuffed man in his overstuffed chair. The sun streamed in through the lace curtains she had made with love and pride several lifetimes ago, causing an absurdly delicate lacy mottling on his all too male face, tee shirt and slacks. The television was on and its pale glow and insidious drone needled into her skin and ears.

I love every extraneous word in that. If you don't, go read Carver.

You Can't Eat the Menu

Being a contrarian often means that you contradict even yourself. I do. Often. As Walt Whitman said more eloquently than I could, "Do I contradict myself? Very well, then I contradict myself, I am large, I contain multitudes."

Now that I've defended purple prose, I caution you that you can't eat the menu. That's not original. I heard it years ago, but I couldn't begin to tell you where. Another version of it is, "The map is not the road". That which symbolizes something is not the thing itself. When stated like this, it seems obvious, but we often mistake the symbol for the thing.

Words are symbols. Plain, pure and simple. That's all they are, really. The symbol can evoke the experience, but it is not the experience. The letters R, E and D, when put together, can make us see something very specific and distinct, but you don't see the color in the word.*

"Yes, Geoff," you say, "this is true. But so what?"

I am a sucker for beautiful language. I love a well put together word image. The words "butterscotch-bright sunlight" evoke an experience for me of a particular type of bright summer day. However, when we create, if we are stuck simply on the beauty of the language, we miss the power of the experience. Like a menu or a map, the words point the way to the experience, but they are not in themselves the experience. Writing should communicate. That's not a rule, of course. Remember what I said about rules.

Don't Leave Your Ego at the Door

I often take to task the people who tell you to "leave your ego at the door" when you come in to a creative session with other writers. For a writer to enter the creative environment having left his ego to wait like an expectant father, sitting on the swing-chair on the porch, is like telling a surgeon to leave his hands on the table outside the operating room so they can't get in anyone's way inside the chest cavity. Okay, perhaps that's not quite an apt analogy, but a writer, any artist, needs an ego in order to think that they have something of value to share with the world. Artists with no ego don't share their work with others, which makes their work almost entirely moot. Unless someone discovers their work and shares it against their wishes.

---

* Yes, I know, you can if the font color is red. Don't be a pill.

This phrase, leave your ego at the door, is meant to make the participants of a creative endeavor get along and be willing to hear and consider the ideas of the others in the room. (It is a phrase also used in many business contexts, and I would submit that it is just as foolish there. Any businessman who builds a business from an idea to a success must have an ego. It is a prerequisite. To tell his underlings to leave their egos at the door would be death to the creativity that got the business to succeed.)

I have another suggestion, although I would hate for it to become so well used as to become a cliché in itself, but why not be focused on the project at hand, and let that be the determining factor, rather than your own self-interests? (Okay, there is little chance that a clumsy sentence like that could become a cliché. So much for being a trend-setter.)

I have a rather large and well developed ego. I like expressing my ideas. I like it when my ideas work, and when they are used. I love it when I get credit for my ideas working and it thrills me to think my ideas might outlast me. However, I am willing to concede that others may also be as brilliant as I am, can come up with ideas as viable as mine and deserve credit when they do. Often, when ego driven people discuss (read: Lock Heads in Mortal Combat) two opposing ideas, if they are at least willing to let the project itself be more important than anyone in the room, a third way will be found that is far better than either of the two ideas being discussed. This is not forgoing your ego. Having the ego had you come up with the original idea that got transformed into the far reaching notion that was finally agreed upon. An ego, your pride, will be better served if the piece works, rather than if "my idea" works. But that doesn't mean you have to repress your ego to make this happen.

Besides, telling an artist to leave his ego at the door is, almost always, an entirely futile and meaningless request. Any artist worth his salt would snap his fingers over his head and say, "Hey, my ego goes where I go, Buddy." Or is that just me?

8
Hope, the Enemy of Art

I hate the word "hope".

I'm going to let that sentence stand there by itself for a moment. In fact, I'll repeat it.

I hate the word "hope".

How can I hate it? The word means looking for a brighter future, it is a vision of a greater life. It is the basis of a political philosophy that desires utopia. Pheh.

When you hope, you immediately give up your power, you immediately give over to the fates your responsibility to do anything more. I hope this will work. I hope I get inspired. I hope they don't mess up the government. I hope I can keep my New Year's resolutions. When most people use the word hope, they've already decided that whatever they hope for probably won't happen. Once that decision is made, it probably won't. "But I am not responsible. After all, I hoped, didn't I? What more can I do?"

Plenty. There is plenty more you can do.

This is very insidious in art. Hope is the enemy of art. I used to tell my acting students, don't hope. Do. Do the work so hope is unnecessary. Do your homework. Do your imagining work. Take control of the process by laying a firm foundation of lived in circumstances and there is no need for hope. I tell you, my fellow writers, the same thing.

When you hope in art, you are telling yourself that there is a possibility that it won't happen. When you give yourself that possibility, you stop being creative. Don't hope. If you need to do something, trust instead. Don't hope your resolutions will work, trust that you created a new year filled with well imagined possibilities. Trust that your vote counts and make sure it's heard, don't hope they will get it right this time. Trust that you can create, that you've done the imaging work, that the work will move you, that the Muse will then whisper in your ear. (Yes, I know. There's no such thing as a Muse. Hush.) That your subconscious mind will provide brilliant, twisted little tidbits for you to play with.

Give up hope. Then do something.

Confusion

There is a philosopher, I forget who, who has a scale of emotions with apathy and depression on the lower end. Confusion is a very high state. I've always thought that questions are much more powerful than answers. We are thrown (like a potter throws clay) to want the answers, but when we have the courage and fortitude to allow ourselves to stay in the question, in the confusion, the Universe opens up for us.

This is relevant for creativity. When we "know" how to do something, when we know the outcome and every piece in between, there is no room for those wonderful little blips that the unconscious loves to throws our way on a project that we've been dwelling on for some time. I like to map out my stories, consider them, design them, if you want to call it that, but when I sit down to write, I am always looking at the story pouring out on my computer screen as if it were something someone else wrote, as if I were reading, as my Mom used to say, "a thumping good piece of literature."

With this as a way of looking at it, the story will often surprise you. Your character will often surprise you and refuse to do what you think they should. Writer Annie Proulx said she'd never experienced characters coming to life in that way and thought it was something writers say to sound mystical. That is until she wrote Brokeback Mountain. She had been imaging Ennis del Mar and Jack Twist for so long and so deeply, with such compassion and emotion, that they did surprise her. She had once called the "falling in love" with your characters "repugnant", but then she wrote that story.

I like going into a project confused, unsure. It's an exciting place to be. I recommend it for anyone who feels they don't have the creative juices to write. Or anyone who does. Having an answer is a stop. There's no need to go further. Asking a question engages your mind, gets you moving and gets you excited. It is almost a hypnotic command to your subconscious. Be confused.

The Myth of the Silver Lining

Contrary to how I often sound, I am an optimist. Many people say that what an optimist does is always "finding the silver lining in every cloud", to find something good in every situation, no matter how dire. This has also been called Pollyanna, after the novel, at least one movie and character of the same name. The young girl in this novel always found something to be glad about in every situation, and her name has come to be used to describe people, usually in slightly derogatory terms, who are blindly optimistic.

And that's the crux of the matter: Blindly optimistic.

I think being blind about anything becomes denying or resisting what is, and resisting what is, as the philosopher said, is the quickest way to unhappiness. Rather than finding the silver lining in everything, I prefer to think of it as finding the opportunity. To do this, we must first acknowledge and tell the truth about what is. Then we can go about finding and exploiting the opportunity. (And there always is one. No matter how hard it is to find.)

This is called solving problems. Solving problems is what makes life interesting. It makes life worthwhile. With no problems to solve, we would be bored out of our heads and not make much of a mark on the planet.

The people we most admire are the people who found big problems and set out to solve them, to greater or lesser degrees of success. Dr. King saw the problem of prejudice and segregation in the South and set out to solve it. Gandhi saw the problems of violence and imperialism in India and set out to solve them. Richard Branson saw the problem of poverty and hunger in Africa and has set out to solve them. The problem must be acknowledged before a solution can be sought.

If all we look for is the silver lining, we'll miss the opportunity.

To bring this all back to the creative process, to the process of writing: As writers, our work is often a reaction to a problem we have witnessed or experienced personally. As writers, our characters must have problems to solve or no one will care. It has been said that drama is conflict. This is also true of comedy, by the way. When a character is presented with a problem, a dilemma, the journey that sends them on is what excites us to write and what excites our readers to read. Even Pollyanna had problems to solve. She saw other people's problems and helped solve them. And if she had never had her crisis of faith, her own self-doubt (her own Gethsemane, to put too much meaning into a children's story) the story would never have become the classic that it did.

Powerful Problems

Many years ago, I took the est training. (Yes, I'm one of those people.) There was one thing they said in it that has stayed with me ever since. Lately I have begun to see it in a different way. The thing is this:

Life is problems. If life is problems, then the way to have a powerful life is to trade your petty (or, perhaps, petit) problems for powerful ones.

An example of a petty problem: How can I come up with rent. An example of a powerful problem: How can I raise a million and a half dollars to make my movie.

Yes, coming up with rent may not seem very petty when you are in the midst of desperate times, but when put against the energy of raising over a million dollars it becomes slightly silly. Other examples of powerful problems: How can I create a foundation dedicated to eradicating poverty in the inner city of Los Angeles. More powerfully, even, than that would be: I now have a deadline of three months to create the foundation.

Even a simple challenge to write every day, which, for many of us, seems almost insurmountable, could become a petty problem when placed against the more powerful one of: I must finish my book proposal and submit it to Random House by the 31st, which brings us to how this whole notion relates to the topic at hand, which is creativity. Making one painting is a petty problem. Filling up a whole gallery showing is much more powerful.

Many of us think we need to progress incrementally, and I often agree with that. I often coach my students that incremental learning is what to focus on, and I still think that's an apt suggestion. However, as I said, I've begun to think of it in different terms. Why not take a quantum leap? Why not set five hurdles in front of yourself rather than one? If you only clear four of them, you're still further along, and you've learned so much more and forced yourself to become a person to be reckoned with.

So look at the problems you are focused on in your life, especially your creative life. See if you can replace them with more powerful problems. Then jump.

Your Reaction To It

In life, and in art, it is not what you are reacting to that matters, it is your reaction to it.

Why do some people breeze through life, seemingly carefree, while others seem to have nothing but bad luck? Is it because only good things happen to them? Is it because they are born to gentler circumstances? I believe it's because they have either learned to, or innately knew from birth, how to react to their circumstances in a powerful, positive way.

There is a play by George S. Kaufman and Moss Hart, You Can't Take It With You, which was made into a movie with Jimmy Stewart, about a man who is engaged to a woman whose family is, shall we say, quirky. They all have very odd passions and odd things happen to them, but they take those odd things in and make them work, somehow. The woman is very embarrassed by her family. The gentleman brings his parents to her family house for dinner on the wrong night because he knows his fiancée would not then have had the time to "fix" her family, and he wanted his family to see the wonderful madness. He realizes that the strangeness of the family is what has shaped the woman he loves into the woman she is. His reaction to them is powerful. He accepts them, embraces them. And they live, we assume, quirkily ever after.

It has been said that the quickest way to be unhappy is to deny what is. If you see something that makes you unhappy, accepting it. Being willing to see it positively can be powerful. (This can be difficult when what you see is horrific, but horrific events are not the norm in most people's lives in Western society. If they are in yours, there is work you must do quite beyond the scope of what I'm talking about in order to remove yourself from these events.)

There are people who live in poverty that see the poverty as their state of being. They generally stay there, or if they are momentarily lifted out, they return. There are people who live in poverty who find or create opportunity in their surroundings despite the poverty, and rise above it. The poverty isn't different in these two cases, the reaction to it is.

What does this have to do with art? I hear many people say that their circumstances are such that they don't have the time or they don't have the freedom or they don't have the support that is needed to create, to write. Nonsense. What they don't have is the willingness to see the circumstances for what they are and write anyway, create anyway.

Does this take work? Sometimes. If you have learned the habit of being crushed by your circumstances, you must find a way to break that habit. There are lots of tools out there to assist you in doing this, more and more every day. Some are better than others, some more effective than others, but all it really takes is a decision to make it work and then any of them will do.

9
The Myth of Perfection

They Can't All Be Gems

Most people who don't write all the time are afraid that, if they do write more, they'll "empty the coffers" very quickly. The logic goes, if it is difficult to come up with something now then make what I come up with brilliant, I'll have nothing left very soon if I try to write more." This is sound logic except for several missing parameters. (How scientific of me!)

Parameter One: There are many ways to come up with ideas that are simple and effective. Gives the lie to the whole premise.

Parameter Two: The more you write, the more in the habit you are of writing. The more in the habit you are of writing, the easier a time your brain will have feeding you ideas. So even if parameter one weren't true, it wouldn't matter.

Parameter Three: You have more ideas than you realize. The only way to get them moving is to get them out. Once you start doing that, it will be a raging flood, which is a completely different, but a much more powerful problem to have.

But most importantly,

Parameter Four: Not everything you write needs to be brilliant. Really. And the more you write, the more chances you have of some of it being brilliant. And the more you write, the more possibilities you have of having something you want to make brilliant even if it's not to begin with.

There goes another excuse not to write. You're welcome.

"But, Geoff," I hear you say. "What do you mean everything you write doesn't need to be brilliant? How can I look myself in the mirror if I produce something sub-par?" (Yes, I can hear you all the way over here in West Los Angeles. You said it very loudly.) What I say to that is, stop requiring brilliance of yourself. At least initially. Just stop it. It feels good to get the yoke off your neck. It is just an excuse not to write. Once you have something down and slightly fleshed out, you can re-awaken your pursuit of excellence and wrestle that puppy into submission. But if you are concerned with excellence the moment you put pen to paper or fingers to keyboard, all you will succeed in doing is stifling yourself.

And, to paraphrase something I once told someone, stop stifling my friend!

(And please forgive me. I feel I've overindulged in metaphor today. Felt good, though. They can't all be gems!)

Premature Judgment

Many writers judge their work too soon in the process. If you think your idea is silly before you've had a chance to really develop it, you've not given it or you a chance. If you think your idea is too dark, take a look at it. There's something there begging to be expressed. If you think the idea has been done before, well, you're right. Everything has been done before. If you worry about that, you'll never write another word. There's nothing new under the sun, to quote Ecclesiastes. It's all been said and done, so you don't have to worry about that one at all. How you say it and do it will be completely distinct from how anyone else said or did it. (Of course, I'm not talking about clichés at all, which in this context is taking an idea and expressing it in a way that has already been expressed, and often. But don't even judge that too soon.)

Some worry about a work's worth before they've even gone through the process of throwing it down on the page. The first draft is just that, a first draft. If you judge yourself while you're writing your first draft, you will never give yourself the freedom to just get the thing down. If you don't give yourself that freedom, you'll never surprise yourself, and if you never surprise yourself, what's the point?

Many writers stop to judge their sentence structure, spelling, word choice before they've even finished imagining the circumstances of the story. What good does that do, besides giving yourself an excuse not to write and to prove (like they always told you) that you have no talent for it? If you think an idea isn't brilliant enough, it never will be. If you think your style isn't smooth enough, it never will be.

Just get your first draft done. Then step away from it for a time (how long depends on the individual. Hours. Days. A week, maybe.) When you come back to it, you can then see what works, what has the potential to work with some adjustment, and what simply doesn't work. This isn't a block of stone, where every hammer blow could make or break it. We can cross things out and write in the margins if we write on paper, or cut, paste, change and delete if we write on the computer.

Subsequent drafts are the time to wrestle the thing to the ground, to find the absolute best word, to worry about grammar and spelling. By that point, you've already given birth to the idea and only at that point is honing it, shaping it, adjusting it appropriate. Only at that point is cutting out what isn't supporting it, trimming what may be too effusive or overburdened with imagery or philosophy going to help you. Only at that point, (if you must) is judging it even remotely productive.

Once you've done your first draft and let it simmer, it is imperative to see what's there and make the necessary adjustments. But if you try to do that before its time, you will kill your art. And if you kill your art, you will kill the desire to create art, which is a tragedy and a crime.

Once you've gotten into the habit of giving yourself and your ideas the freedom of an unrestricted first draft, you will notice, with each piece, that you find less and less that needs adjusting on the subsequent drafts.

Good Enough

I talk a lot about perfection and how it will thwart you every time. Writer James Thurber said, "Don't get it right, get it written." Musician Pat O'Bryan said, "You can work on an album until it's perfect. And dead." James Agee started writing A Death in the Family in 1948. He was still revising it in 1955 when he died. It was published posthumously.

If you are striving for excellence, to achieve the best you can within the constraints you have, this is worthy of art. If you are waiting for perfection to share your work with the world, it will never happen. We are imperfect creatures and, as many native people around the world believe, if we attempt perfection or profess perfection, we risk offending God.

I'm not talking about mediocrity. Mediocrity, of course, is an enemy of art. Often we are afraid that, if we let a piece just be good enough rather than perfect, it will be mediocre. Nonsense. The Icelandic people have a proverb: "Mediocrity is climbing molehills without sweating". It is not striving for anything. A writer, an artist, must strive for something worthwhile, but get the work in good shape, get it to say what you need it to say, and say that smoothly, then move on. Good enough is good enough when weighed against perfection.

Let us not be James Agee. Had he been satisfied with good enough, he would have seen A Death in the Family become a best seller and would have been able to feed his family. And it still would have been a great book.

Obsessive Much?

I often talk about the need to get stuff done as opposed to getting it done perfectly. The whole, "do you want it perfect or do you want it on Tuesday" philosophy is an apt one. Besides the notion that perfect isn't possible, it can drive one crazy when one tries to reach it. Okay, full disclosure. I am often, not always but often, such a one.

And it hath, as Hamlet said to Ophelia, made me mad. At least a little. I start out with all good intentions striving for excellence, but balancing that against the reality of getting something done and done on time. (As long as we are confessing things, I must tell you that as I get older "on time" has become a much more fluid a concept.)

The Internet has changed the way I do things. I used to slave over every detail until the project went out, then leave all mistakes in the hands of my betters. Now, I get something done, post it on whatever site it is being posted on, then obsess about it. Reread it. Tweak it. Worry over it. I have spent the last two days putting up a site for a project that a friend and I am doing which sells fine hand-crafted jewelry among other things. She is in charge of the jewelry and I'm in charge of writing and designing the site and the sales system. I obsessed about every detail and finally finished the site sometime yesterday. My friend, Laureen, loved it, but made a couple of suggestions. I added those. Now I have spent the entire day... the ENTIRE day, going back and fixing, tweaking, adjusting, doctoring, revamping, honing and making it generally but oh so subtly better.

I do the same thing when I write. I reread it over and over after I've decided it was done. When Steve Mancini and I used to post chapters to our on-line serial (that became our book, Weeping Willow) I would spend the entire evening rereading the chapter eight or ten times, often going back in and making "just one" tiny adjustment. Eight or ten times. Steve makes fun of me. Once it's done, he is willing to declare it done. "Are you reading it again!?!" "Yes. Shut up."

This stuff makes it better. Does it make it perfect? No. Does it mean I'm crazy? Probably.

I am obsessive. Is there something wrong with that?

I certainly hope not.

Important Work

The other side of the "Good Enough" conversation is the notion of art as "Important Work". Recently, I was thinking about the phrase, "an important work" by "an important writer" and wondered if any of my stuff will ever be important. Then I realized it already is. So is yours. Nothing you write will have ever been said in quite the same way, with quite the same voice by anyone else. (Unless, of course, you copy it directly from another author, in which case it isn't writing, it's transcribing and is considered bad form.)

We have all been taught, here in Western society, that we aren't important, that, on some level, we don't count. (Conversely we have also been taught that the individual is all, therefore we are the most important person in the world. This psychological dichotomy is fascinating and explains much about the American dilemma, but not the thrust of this bit, so I'll leave it there.) As artists (and we are all artists, aren't we?) we are important. Art, creativity, is what keeps the society alive, keeps it thriving, therefore it is not a leap of logic to say that, when you create art, it is, by definition, important.

This is all a philosophic statement, of course. Are we all Shakespeare or Whitman? Are we Wyeth or Balanchine? No, of course not. Most of us won't reach those heights (although not considering your work important will go a long way towards assuring that you don't.) Many of our works will not be seen by masses of people, but they will be seen by some, and will affect, perhaps influence and change, those people that do view them, which makes them important if nothing else does.

Ultimately, whether you are important or not doesn't really matter, but if you believe you aren't, you will keep yourself from creating art and that's a tragedy.

Perfectionists Unite

I mean no irony when I say I am a recovering perfectionist. Anyone who has ever slogged through any of my first drafts (and often second and third drafts) will be surprised to hear that. I have never applied that bit of psychological dogma to spelling, (or housekeeping) but it is, or at least has been, a constant cause of frustration and awe.

I've talked a lot about perfection. There is a big difference between the pursuit of perfection and of excellence. You can be excellent in whatever you pursue, but you can't be perfect. To attempt it is a losing battle.

There are even those who say that perfection is death, that you will only be perfect in the moment of your death, but even that seems a stretch. What if I die in some ignoble way? Hit by a diaper delivery truck, say, or from complications resulting from a hangnail or choking on a Twinkie? I can hear the comments now. "Well, that's just perfect."

So how do you avoid the attempt of reaching perfection? Don't try to do it perfectly. Take it in small steps. As you sit down to describe something tell yourself, "for this time, just for the next five minutes, I have permission to be sloppy". Give yourself that permission. It will free you up. It will actually feel good. Revel in your sloppiness, your glorious imperfections, as you write. You may even be surprised at what you produce once you're not so concerned with its perfection. You might also not be surprised, or you might be surprised at how supremely imperfect it actually seems. If you aren't trying for perfection, this is okay, and you can continue. You stop using perfection as an excuse to not get things done.

Another trick to try is to realize that you will never make the perfect choice. There is never a perfect choice, there is only the one you chose. When confronted with two or more things, just choose. Yes, do your due diligence. Do whatever thought and research and preliminary work you need to, but know that, once the decision has been made, the only correct answer to "Why did you choose that?" is, "Because I did." It's not the perfect choice. It is simply the one you made. And that is powerful and freeing.

Yes, I know. I have contradicted this often when writing and directing. I have demanded perfection or as near as was possible from myself and those around me. I will probably do it again. Hey, I'm a human. Nobody's perfect.

Not everything you write will be brilliant. But if you don't write anything, nothing will be brilliant. Not everything you write will work on all levels, but you have to put it out there. The bottom of your dresser drawer can't be enlightened. Share your work!

Every time you sit down to write, give yourself permission to be sloppy. To be imperfect. To be disjointed and incoherent. The more you write, the more you will be amazed at how much you have to say.

Part Two

What to Do About Them

10
The Power of Possibility

In this section of the book, I'm going to talk a lot about my experience, my process. There will be tidbits there that will suggest ways you can create your process. A lot of what works for me will work for you. I recommend imagining yourself with those experiences, or with the process I'm discussing. This will help you find for yourself things you hadn't yet thought of to excite your own writing process.

A blank piece of paper (or a curser blinking on a blank screen) can be the most wonderful of things. It can fill you with wonder or dread. I chose wonder. The possibilities are endless. Shall I create a lush landscape and people it with gnomes? Shall it be a bleak forest full of gnarled, sickly trees covered in stringy moss or a gleaming city with tall buildings, fast automobiles and faster people hurrying toward their dreams?

I conjure, more powerfully than any wizard or mage, dark realms and bright, a farm with simple people tending strange beasts, a ramshackle hut filled with the smell of wood smoke and roasting meat, a dark spaceship hurtling toward the horizon of imagination.

I write because of the power it gives me to create whole worlds and explore others, to breathe life, godlike, into new beings. I write because of the gift of being able to bring other people along on my journey.

And in creating, I am created. To paraphrase Descartes, I write, therefore I am. Writing allows me to examine my psyche, to justify my existence, to explore my doubts and triumphs.

I stare at the blank piece of paper (or the curser blinking on the blank screen) and I am spellbound with awe at the possibilities.

Why Art?

I know people who would rather not be challenged in their lives. They prefer a comfortable job and, as musician Pat O'Bryan calls it, a McLife. It's valid. It has confuses me, but, as the philosopher said, confusion is a very high state and understanding is the booby prize, so I don't need to understand it, I just need to accept it.

It's valid, but it's not for me and never has been. I've held jobs often in my life, but always considered them a way to support my habit of creating art. (An often very bad habit, I assure you, much like smoking, but without all the ashes and nicotine stains.)

I have also long been amazed (I first started noticing it when I was in junior high school) at many American's pride in their own ignorance. They want to be ignorant, and distrust those who aren't. I don't say all Americans, or any one class of Americans, but I see it as a very large portion of my fellow citizens. Again, it confuses me. I am so passionate about wanting to know everything about everything, I don't get people who don't want to know anything about anything.

Again, I suppose, it's valid. Most of us have come from peasant stock, and the way to survive as a peasant is to lay low, not be noticed and do as you're told. That's what you do, and that's what you teach your children. The prairie dog that pops his head above ground it the one most likely to be grabbed by the eagle to become a lovely snack. I absolutely come from peasant stock, so it would seem that I should also want to lay low, but I also come from parents who questioned, examined and wanted to shake things up, so I inherited some of that, too. I like to cause ripples. (I do it nicely, of course. Usually.) One of the best ways to cause ripples, to question, to shake things up, is through art. With art, it can be done either didactically or subtly. I've used both. (Yes, believe it or not, I can be subtle.) Subtlety usually works better. Don't make a rule about that.

There will always be people who are bosses and always be people who are employees. How could we have bridges and power stations and West End theatres and the Internet if that weren't so? However, and I've said this before, I think that art, the creation of it and the consumption of it in all of its messy iterations, is what makes a society live, thrive. The bridges and power stations and theatres are just the trappings, the tools needed for society to function and survive. In order for it to thrive, there is art.

In this day of mass media, the Internet, social networking, etc., the peasants have been given the keys to the castle in a way not ever seen in history.

Only some of them (us) will accept the keys. This is valid. I want my own set.

The Power of Art

I had a conversation with a friend in high school, sometime back during the Lincoln administration, about art and society. She was a talented piano player and singer who was becoming disenchanted with art. She said that, with everything that was going on in the world, it seemed to her a life pursuing art was a pointless life, that there was so much more that was so much more important to do. My comment then was that a society without art is a dead society and, therefore, pursuing art might be the most important thing one could do; assuring the preservation of society itself. (My friend, by the way, ended up going to Juilliard, so she seemed to have gotten past her disenchantment.)

I still feel that way.

This is not just an empty, philosophical stance. Consider that one of the first things the Nazis did when they came to power was declare which art was sanctioned and which art was "decadent". What they considered decadent was anything that showed any creative or original voice, not necessarily things that were sexual or salacious, as the word decadent might imply. Art is often considered dangerous by totalitarian governments or dogmatic people. Again, not necessarily only art that questions policy, incites dissent or demands change, but any art that questions anything because questions cause thinking and thinking is very dangerous. That's the kind of danger I'm attracted to.

Art has the power change everything, to preserve everything, to question everything. It can provoke thought, emotion, action. It can express the inability to act. It can funnel great mourning and great joy. It can tell the truth and can both tell and expose the great lie. It can also simply entertain, which is no small thing.

So. I don't know if what I do is the most important thing I could do, but it is close to the only thing I can do so what's to be done? Even in those moments when I despair, which are rarer as I grow older, I remind myself that what I do is contributing to the evolution of the mind of man and I find some peace.

Can Art Change a Life?

On a radio show recently the question was put forth, "does art have the power to change a life?" Although I've always thought a life without art is a dead life and a society without art is a dead society, I'd never considered the question quite in that way. It started me thinking about my own journey.

I graduated from college with a Bachelor of Arts degree in theatre. The plan after college was to spend a year in Northern California with my brother and his wife while getting acclimatized to life outside of school, then move to San Francisco and disappear into some rep company or other and spend my days happily ensconced in a life in theatre.

I often visited San Francisco with my brother and sister-in-law, seeing plays, visiting museums, drinking in the Bohemia of it all, preparing for my eventual move there. As Robert Burns said to the wee mouse, "The best-laid schemes o' mice an' men/Gang aft agley..." Okay, so my schemes weren't all that well laid out to begin with, but they did gang a bit agley.

Soon after lighting in Northern California, I got a job at the Round Table Pizza parlor at Brunswick Plaza, half way between the small towns of Grass Valley and Nevada City. I was quickly promoted to assistant manager and moved into a tiny house in Grass Valley. I didn't have a car, almost everything I needed I could get to by walking or riding my ten-speed bike. Everything but movies. There was one movie theatre that served both towns. It had three screens and was fairly close to me, but their usual fair tended to ooze a little too much testosterone for my taste. The nearest alternative was in Sacramento, a forty-five minute drive down the highway. If I wanted to see something that didn't have Sylvester Stallone in it I would need to find someone else who wanted to go who also had a car.

Poppycock!

One afternoon I decided I needed to see a movie but no one I knew wanted to go. My friend Vern, however, who lived right across the street from me, offered the use of his car. I decided on The China Syndrome, which was playing at one of the bigger complexes in the outskirts of Sacramento, gathered up the keys and journeyed hence.

The movie, starring Jane Fonda, Michael Douglas, Jack Lemmon and Wilford Brimley, was a political thriller very loosely based on the Three Mile Island incident. A young, naive reporter (Fonda) accidentally stumbles upon evidence that the safety inspections for the building of the local nuclear plant were fudged and those responsible ranged from the halls of corporations to the government. The script was tight, the direction flawless. The tension built slowly but steadily to a fever pitch. Jack Lemmon, an actor I always admired, was never better. I was moved. Stunned might be a better world. On the ride home in that borrowed car, I decided I wanted to be part of an industry that could produce something so powerful. The next day I put my notice in at the pizza parlor.

I saw the movie two more times that week, convincing friends they had to go. None of them seemed as moved as I was, but they humored me. It wasn't until the third viewing that I realized that there was no background music in the film, only incidental music occasionally coming from a car radio or in a party scene. How tight must a movie be to not rely on music to manipulate your emotions? How courageous must a director be to make that choice? If I'd had any doubts about my impending relocation, they vanished.

I bought a car, a Ford Grand Torino station wagon, bright orange, loaded all my belonging in back and literally a month after that initial viewing of the movie I was on my way to Los Angeles. I lived in the car those first few days, parking on side streets in this unfamiliar town, until I tracked down some friends from college and camped out on their living room couch. I stayed with them until I found a small room in a building just north of Hollywood Boulevard, got a job at an answering service and became a Los Angelian. Before watching that movie, it was completely unpredictable that I move to this town, one I'd never even visited. I liked San Francisco. Whenever I visited there, it felt like home, yet here I am. I tell people I was headed for San Francisco but took a wrong toin at Albuquoique.

That was in 1979. My acting dreams have transformed, I am now a writer, but I still live quite happily and productively in Los Angeles after all these years, working in and around the industry that made such a powerful film. I look upon that evening in a movie house in Sacramento as a major turning point in my life.

To answer the question posed by the radio show, yes, I say. Art does have the power to change one's life. I often wonder what that original trail would have been like, but the one I chose has thus far been wildly diverting.

Passion

Passion has always been my favorite word (well, maybe not always, I suspect when I was a kid, it was more like "fun" and when I was a teenager, it was more like "angst" but, hey, I'm an old fogy now and if I say always, take it how you like it.)

I love when people discover their passion. Or passions. I love when people start moving toward their passion. It moves me to watch people grow as they realize that they can live from their passion. I have many passions, but almost all of them revolve around creativity. When I taught an acting class, it was called Passion for Acting. One reason I started this book was because of my passion for writing and the writing process.

11
Write. Right?

I recently had a conversation with a friend of mine who said she said she loved writing but didn't write much because she didn't think she had anything to say. It is a comment I have heard often and it makes me sad. I take extreme exception to that comment whenever I hear it.

You do have something to say. Everyone does. Everyone has a story. Everyone has several. Everyone has had experiences that would communicate with or intrigue or enlighten or motivate or piss off other people. Any one of those responses (plus a million others I could list if I wanted) are more than valid and more than reason enough to write.

So you haven't gotten to the point where you have the "answers", yet, and you know that what people want are the answers. Well, a philosopher once said, "understanding is the booby-prize". My personal take on that is that the question is much more powerful than the answer. When you are "living in the question", your life is a journey. If you think you've found the answer, your journey is at an end. The journey is what is exciting and interesting, not the destination.

So bring people along on your journey. Write about what questions you are examining in your life, about what trials life has set before you to conquer. Write about the lessons you have learned along the way, yes, but also about the new questions that come up as you move forward. Write about the defeats, the triumphs, the confusions, the tentativeness, the certainty that you experience on a day-to-day basis. Write about those moments when what you were certain of suddenly becomes less certain, when it becomes a new question.

Our journeys are what make us human, not the destination. (It could be argued that the ultimate destination is death, so if you're waiting to write until you "get there", it may be entirely too late by then.) Our journeys also are what make us interesting. We all love to read about other people's journeys. We would love to read about yours.

You do have something to write about. When you think you don't, breathe in, close your eyes for a moment and thank that thought, then open them back up again and start writing. If you can't think of anything else to write about, write about not having anything to write about. The journey is everything.

What Do You Mean, You're Not Writing?

I love being creative. That's not much of a surprise for anyone who knows me, but I do. When I really start creating, when I really start listening to those voices who are giving me the ideas to write down, I start feeling a mixture of a deep satisfaction, slightly embarrassing pride, a vague but exciting antsy anticipation in my stomach, right next to that ball of warmth. And I can't wait to share what I'm creating.

There are different kinds and levels of creativity. I have spent the last several days creating a new training course with a book, worksheets and video instruction, all the while thinking, "As soon as I'm done, here, I can go be creative." But a funny thing happened. Today I suddenly noticed that mixed up feeling. Where did that come from? Oh, yeah. Creating that course. I needed to pull from my experience, delve into my knowledge. I had to imagine what the student would need, put myself there. Instinctively (translated: from deep habit) I used my senses to do so.

I posed circumstance and questions that I trusted my subconscious would provide the answers to and lived through the struggles of my imagined students. Then I waited a little while as it percolated (and, as is also my habit, a little while as I procrastinated) then jumped in and followed the story that had been born, almost complete like Athena who leapt fully formed from Zeus' forehead. (He must have been imagining her for a very long time! Well, maybe it was Metis who did the imagining. Look it up.) It all sounds sort of like what I go through when I'm writing a story. It almost sounds like creativity. No wonder I'm feeling so smug!

In any case, once the product is done and out, I can get back to the latest novel, but I'm already being creative, so my soul seems content.

This Book Is Not Really About Sex

I keep being pulled away from what I want to do (write, act, direct, create ephemera that is lasting) and into what I need to do (make a living, pay bills, fulfill commitments, be a friend.) The dream is to mesh the two into one glorious existence, but I haven't yet found the wit or endurance to make that work entirely. There are bleak moments when I think that will never happen. Then I'll sit down and write something that astonishes me and remember why I am trying to make a living, pay bills, fulfill commitments and be a friend. It is to be able to exist in a world where I can write, act, direct and create ephemera that is lasting.

    And somehow, I'm sure, all this has something to do with sex, although that is only a vague notion brought on by the vague awareness of sex at the edges of my consciousness most moments I'm awake. Of course, there is also a vague awareness of death that lingers nearby, so it may also have something to do with that. Most of what I create has one or both of those hovering about the edges, so I'll assume for the moment everything does.

    I wrote a short story, dark and surreal with odd and oddly obvious symbolism, several years ago after a cross country road trip, about a man who wakes up in a nondescript, slightly decrepit motel room who doesn't know who he is, where he has come from or where he is headed. He only knows what he can see and sense around him, the cigarettes, his wallet, his dirty fingernails, the musty smell in the room, and from these concludes that he's traveling. By the end, he isn't even astonished to find himself fading into the mattress. Most people would find this story bleak. The first few people I showed it to found reading it very uncomfortable. I have a very different relationship to it, however. I find it having been an empowering exercise to write and a rewarding one to read. I am delighted to have created (or transcribed, it doesn't matter which) that bleak moment.

    When I start feeling like the direction of my life has been diverted by dams, culverts, flumes and groynes I remember a poem that delighted me in childhood or I read about a young writer that is taking the world by the short and curlies or I remember one of my own stories that delighted me in the telling and I know that, no matter what direction the river is flowing, what is slowing it or changing its course, it always ends up at the sea and it makes my heart sing and my body want to sit down and write something.

For those who like to see behind the curtain, today the remembered poem was Eletelephony by Laura Richards, the young writer is Christopher Stoddard and the story is called The Ephemera, which you can find on Amazon.com.

The Death of Books, Newspapers, Apple Pie and Everything?

Everyone is talking about the death of books and of traditional publishing and publishers. We watched newspapers struggle in the wake of information readily available on the Internet, now we're seeing publishing houses scramble in the wake of Amazon's print-on-demand and Author's Centers services, etc.

I had a conversation about this with a friend of mine and thought I'd share some of what we discussed with you. My friend had been in the newspaper biz and lost his job, perhaps because of the downsizing of his paper, perhaps for other reasons, and the whole thought of the possible disappearance of major publishers startles him.

I have been saddened by the diminishing of so many newspapers, especially in the area of arts coverage. One of the reasons I started one of my sites, a theatre review site, was because the LA Times had stopped reviewing small theatre in LA and the small theatres were dying. But being sad about it is one thing. I also realize that I get most of my news from the Internet. As in all the other disciplines, there are papers that are thriving because they've embraced the new way of disseminating information rather than resisting it.

I actually can't imagine big-time publishers all going away. The ones who don't embrace the new way of things may go, but I personally would love to have a huge house behind me who believes in me and pushes my stuff. I am also enough of a realist (that has come late in my life, unfortunately) to know that, unless I'm Stephen King or J.K. Rowling, (or even Joe Vitale) even if they do publish me, I will have to do all the work to get the word out.

I don't think Amazon, or any of the other such on-line services, are trying to do away with the big publishers. It would be suicide for them. What they are doing is slowly and methodically creating ways for writers to take control of their own work. Even if that work is published by one of the big guys. This, as far as I can see, is a very good thing.

And I really don't think physical books are going away. I personally love them too much. I have walls of books in almost every room in my house. I can't see a wall of Kindles. Wouldn't have the same effect at all.

The old ways of doing things will have to adjust to the new, that's all. It happened to music (is still happening to music!) and the labels are finally catching up. It is also happening to movies. Again, I don't think most of the labels or the studios will go away, but the model will have to change for them, too. I personally resisted the whole eBook thing, but I've published several of my own on Kindle. Yes, I love the look and feel and heft and smell of a real book. But I love to read and I can carry hundreds of books in my pocket on my iPhone Kindle app.

Digital delivery isn't killing books any more than photography killed paintings or television killed movies or radio killed records or MTV killed radio or Disco killed music. It all just evolves.

12
Putting Off Procrastination

    This whole book to this point has simply been examining the fact that writers often find the most creative excuses not to write. We will use anything from messy desks to low biorhythms to avoid getting down to business. Creativity is fragile, we think, and we mustn't jostle it. I am as guilty of this as anyone. (We often write what we need to learn.) And I know that creativity isn't fragile at all, it's hale and robust, practically indestructible if you feed it well, but thinking of it as dainty is a convenient myth when I'm looking for an excuse.

    I check my email. I check to see if anyone has responded to any of my Facebook or Twitter posts. I think of something clever to post on Twitter that will also show up on Facebook, which will give me an excuse to go back and check both of them again in a few minutes. I drink the last of the coffee and must make more. I fuss with my computer settings, telling myself that, in doing so, I'm making myself more productive. I fuss with my calendar settings, telling myself the same thing. (Excuses are elastic and adaptable, it seems.)

I have had two conversations in the past week about this habit of procrastination. It wasn't until the first one that I recalled the length of time I have been a willing slave to it. As a grade school kid, I avoided picking up my text books, avoided sitting down to do my math or history homework, until it was often simply too late.

Once I remembered this, I started looking at what the mechanism was and it seems I want to avoid anything that feels, however irrationally, like it will be too difficult or complicated. Also, I fear doing something that seems it might be what is known as mind-numbingly boring or repetitious. I also notice that when I dive into something, no matter how complicated it is (or how boring), I am very good at figuring it out and getting it done, so the thoughts that come up to trigger my procrastination have little or no basis in reality. Imagine that. What a surprise.

With this new observational viewpoint, I started to put a task on my daily calendar and knew I would get to it and get it done. For example, I've been whining for months that I have a new idea for a novel that I wanted to write, but had no time to actually write it. I went on and on about how busy I was and won't it be nice when I finally have the luxury of time to sit down and be creative rather than spin my wheels making a living. Well, now I have it on my daily calendar: "One hour a day, work on Old Magic".

Now, when the old thoughts come up, so does an annoying green reminder that in five minutes I need to be working on my book and I open the document and start working. It's not brilliant every morning, but there's no possibility of brilliance showing up if I'm not doing anything at all, so I let it be ugly and mundane and pedestrian and keep writing. It seems to be working.

Now I have to check my email, Facebook and Twitter pages.

The Best Time to Write

I used to be a night person. I was in the theatre, after all. (And, yes, I spell it with and "re". I'm pretentious and gay.) Even in college, when most people were getting up at dawn to get to their first class sometime in the prehistoric and mythological hours of seven or eight in the morning, the earliest class I ever had in the entire four years was at ten. But I wasn't goldbricking, I often didn't get home from rehearsal until after midnight, then had to do homework. I did my best writing in the afternoon, when the sun was just shining through the leaves of the trees on the commons, dappling the lawn and my thoughts.

When I first came to Los Angeles, I got a job at the switchboard of the Pacific Theatre Corporation (see? I'm not the only one with the "re" thing.) I worked the evening shift. The phone pretty much stopped ringing after my first hour there, then didn't pick up until well after midnight when all the theatres started calling in to report their box office receipts, which I would record for a report that went on all the executives' desks first thing in the morning. From about seven until midnight there was little to do in the bleak solitude of the little office where the PBX phone was. Most on that shift watched a small black and white television that sat in the corner of the desk. Some read. I wrote a novel. Evenings, it seemed, were my most creative time.

In my thirties, I discovered Julia Cameron's The Artist's Way and doing the 12 week odyssey she outlined in that wonderful book changed the way I viewed creativity. One of the first exercises she laid out was the Morning Pages; spending ten or fifteen minutes in the morning, right after you awaken (and after any necessary trip to the john) writing long-hand in a stream-of-consciousness journal. I poured my mind out every morning and discovered several short stories lurking in those pages. Mornings were definitely the best time for me.

When I first started blogging regularly I wrote a blog post every morning. Then writing started to get later and later in the day until it threatened to overtake dinnertime, so I decided to write the blogs the night before to be ready to post first thing in the morning. The pressure was gone and the quiet sounds of the cars speeding by on Washington Boulevard lulled me into a pleasant state of creative bliss. I have been amazed at some of the words that flow from my fingers onto the screen.

So. What is the best time to write? When you do. And as often as possible.

It's Complicated

Some people are in the habit of making simple things complicated. People who do this probably won't recognize themselves in that sentence, however. For them, it's just how things are. So are you one of these closet complicators?

Answer these questions:
- Do you ever notice that, when someone says "it's easy," your first reaction is, "sure it is."
- Does it take you a lot longer to complete a task than it does other people?
- Have you ever turned a one-step process into a ten-step process, even if it was because the one-step process just wasn't good enough?
- If someone suggests that you alphabetize a group of objects by letter, do you first decide that there are several things the objects could be called, so you devise a way to determine what the actual

name of the object is before you begin alphabetizing?
- If someone asks you the time, do you supply the history of watches, just to make sure you're answering the question completely?
- Are you really frustrated that there are only 7 questions because that isn't nearly enough to determine anything?

And finally:
- Do people ever tell you that you've made something more complicated than you need to?

If you answered yes, or even "I'll have to think about it" to any of these questions, then I'm talking about you. It is especially so if you answered "well, I sort of do one or two of them, but I don't do the other ones, so that might mean I could say yes or no to the original premise, which is really much too simplistic to begin with so I think what I'm going to do is create my own set of questions and answer them, then maybe send my questions to Geoff because they would be a much better indication of someone being driven to complicate things, unlike the very incomplete set of questions he's using now. I wonder who he's talking about, anyway. Maybe I should send this to my husband, he always complicates things."

So. We've established that you complicate things. (Full disclosure, I am often guilty of several of these, so I'm right with you on this one.) What's to be done? Well, as the Friends of Bill say, the first step is acknowledging you have a problem. There is help out there. Once you've acknowledged it, step back, breathe in once or twice, then really look at what the original instruction was and just do what the original instruction was, not what you think it should have been. (Notice I said breathe in once or twice, I didn't say start a meditation ritual that includes breathing.)

Once you begin to notice you complicate things, simplifying them can be quite easy. When you notice that you've done it again (and you will, when you have that habit it doesn't disappear in a day even if we want it to disappear in a day) don't get mad at yourself, that's counterproductive. Instead, just say, "Oh, isn't that interesting, there it is again. Well, what do I do now? Now I remind myself to be simple." It takes all the energy off of it. If you want you can even add a step called "Laugh, because we do cling to things," but be careful. Don't add any more steps than that or you're back into it.

How does this relate to writing? Many people get frustrated by writing because they try to make it much too complicated, especially at the beginning: They try to include every detail of every circumstance. They think it must be grand and brilliant, so they spin their wheels adjusting and enhancing things way too early in the process. If you do this, stop, breathe in a couple of times, then simply get on paper what's in your head and only what's in your head at that moment. Once you've done that, you can adjust, add detail and make it brilliant. At that point, you can even complicate it if you feel the need, because, at that point, you've already written, so it won't stop you from writing.

This is Just Terrible!

When Steve Mancini and I write together, at least once during every project Steve will lament, "There's no story, there's nothing going on, there's no conflict, it's not funny!" He's only partly joking when he does it. No matter how much thought, imagination, preparation and care we've put into the project, there is often a point where one or both of us think it's just not good and just not repairable. Thankfully, we're both aware of this and one of us will remind the other that it's all just part of the process, so just shut up and get on with it. The moment usually passes fairly quickly.

It's easier to believe in and get caught up in that thought process when you're writing on your own, however. I know. I went through it this morning while working on Old Magic. I have been working a lot on the characters, especially the main fellow, whose name is Samuel. I've been building him from the ground up, spending time with him, getting to know him. He's a little more irascible now than I imagined he would be but in spite of that, I like him. This morning I sat down to type out some notes of things that had occurred to me in the last day or so that I hadn't yet gotten down and started getting a little ahead of myself. (Yes, I often do what I teach my students to look out for. I know these things because I've experienced them.) I started worrying how I was going to logically build to a specific plot point that was large, necessary and important to the point of the whole story. And I thought, "This story won't work."

I sat back, disgruntled. (Have you ever been gruntled?)

Then I remembered that I wasn't there, yet, that it was too soon to worry about that and by the time I was there I will have done sufficient work living in the world that the thrust of the story will simply unfold before me. I got over myself and went back to the keyboard.

I wonder, though, how many writers get to that point and really think it means something other than that they've gotten to that point in the process, the point where they're questioning their sanity for pursuing the project, and let it stop them. I wonder how many very worthwhile projects are simply abandoned before they've had the opportunity to breathe with a vibrant life of their own because the writer had never been told to simply thank those thoughts of self-doubt, declare them a crucial part of the process and get back to work.

That little moment of drama in my writing session today, that doubt that I'll be able to connect the dots, will likely seep down into my subconscious like nitrogen-rich water and fertilize a whole garden of rich fruit for me to encounter after turning a corner one day while strolling through my modern day fictionalized Los Angeles in my mind. I won't try to dictate now what I'll discover there. But I'm very excited to discover it.

Indefensible English

People who know me (and, I suspect, many who don't) know that I am a terrible speller. I used to say I could have the word "cat" three times in a sentence and it wouldn't look the same twice. An exaggeration, to be sure, but it makes the point. My mother used to tell me "just sound it out". This resulted in some very interesting words appearing on my pages. (Did you know that the word you speak as "vittles" is actually spelled, "victuals"? How the hell did that happen?)

I remember in college a meeting with my English professor, Sister Jean Concannon, talking about one of the short stories I'd submitted. She mentioned the spelling. (Remember, this was sometime during the Lincoln administration. Personal computers hadn't been invented, yet, thus, no spell check.) She told me I that, if I should need to know how to spell a word, I should simply look it up in the dictionary. Then she noticed the conflicted look on my face, laughed and told me of a former student to whom she had suggested the same thing, who had teared up and asked, "How can I look it up if I don't know how to spell it?" At that moment, I felt understood.

I can type a word in such a convoluted way that I totally flummox spell-check. I can sit for long stretches, trying different permutations until I can find something that the poor program can at least recognize as an English word so that it can give me some idea of how to proceed. (It would probably help if I didn't insist on using words like "permutations". However, 1. I find I can spell those words much more easily than more simple ones, and 2. I like those words.)

Lately, I've found that Google has become quite a good spell-checker. If my handy, tried and true WordPerfect can't parse a word for me, other than to indicate with a squiggly red line that it is unrecognizable, typing my unrecognizable word into Google will often lead me to the correct (or at least A correct) spelling.

Another teacher that I studied with in my late forties said, "English is indefensible." He was teaching us a technique for remembering the correct spelling of words, using (I now go to Google for a moment) Albuquerque as an example. It was a plausible technique, but one I have yet to master. That you can't defend English, however, was a revelation. I finally relaxed as I saw just how true this is. When I'm writing with Steve Mancini, I'm usually the one at the keyboard, and when I type a word incorrectly, it prickles Steve's sense of decorum and he will let me know that the word should be corrected before we can move on. Lately, I've been asking him, "why is it spelled that way?" Usually, he comes back with a shy smile and a shrug and some variation of "English is indefensible."

It isn't only the spelling, either. Our language is rich and varied, one of the reasons I love playing in it so much. This richness, this lush expanse of vernacular possibilities, comes in part because we've borrowed words, thoughts and meanings from so many different sources. How else could you explain the conflict between the meanings of "salt of the earth" and "salting the earth". One is a very good thing, the other is decidedly not, yet the actual phrases only exchange an "i-n-g" with a "space-o-f".

Because we've taken so much from so many sources, sometimes adjusting it to match our "rules", sometimes not, our language can be very confusing. I have, however, realized I quite like the confusion of it, from chaos comes creativity, and find I have no need whatsoever to defend it.

Poppycock!

And the more at peace I become with the fact that "that's just the way it is", the better my spelling is becoming.

All this is to point out that, while you're writing, don't stop to correct your spelling. Or your grammar. Or anything. Once you get it all set down, go back and correct it. Premature worry about use of proper English will stop you from writing every time.

13
Getting Started

I mentioned in the first section that I have a habit, bad or good, I've no idea, where, once I've written something, I read over it several times, almost obsessively, trying to imagine what some other reader would think of it. I'm not sure why I do this, and I've always felt at least a little silly about it, but there it is.

Last night I finished the first draft of the prologue of a new novel. It's not long as prologues go, and from experience the chance that it will end up exactly the way it is in the final product are slim, but after I'd written the last moment, which I had been quite excited to get to, I immediately started reading it from the top. Each time I went through it I tweaked a bit, changing a description, adding detail, correcting a word or a spelling, but the tweaking wasn't why I reread it.

As I said, I had been very excited to get to that last moment while writing it out and I think I wanted to assure myself that I had led up to it properly, that it was sufficiently startling. Getting to that moment was why I'd actually started writing it at all. I've been doing a lot of background work for the novel, imagining people and places, deciding on conflicts, living through the cycles and thrusts of the story, both viscerally and philosophically, but the starting off point, the thing that propelled the story into motion had been missing. Last night I realized that I had it, that it had been there for a few days without my knowing it, so I sat down and wrote what lead up to that moment. In the process, my two main characters started breathing a bit more.

As I write, when I write like that, when the story is becoming complete somewhere in my subconscious, I know where it's headed (of course I do) but on some odd level I experience the writing as if I were reading someone else's story for the first time and I want to see how it turns out. That's not completely accurate, but I'm not sure I can describe it exactly. I can say that, when I've done good preliminary groundwork building, writing it down is, or at least can be, a thrilling experience. Perhaps one of the reasons I reread a piece so often right after I've finished it is to keep that feeling alive longer before it inevitably fades.

In any case, as I reread it, I decided that I liked it. That it is a fine beginning, as far as it goes. That it nicely sets things up, but in a way that isn't obvious. I don't think that moment, the one I was so keen to get to, is nearly as startling as I'd thought it would be, but I also now think it needn't be.

Now I need to complete the groundwork for the next bit, which is rapidly getting to the point in my head where it must also be put down.

Make Writing a Job

I've talked before about scheduling writing, treating it as a job, but even I forget my own advice sometimes. I used to say I was pining for the day when I had the luxury to write the book that has been forming in my head for several months.

When I got the idea, I jotted down several notes, then went away, sad that I had to wait to write it.

Then I got around to setting up the time management system I mentioned in the last chapter. I've been keeping to that time commitment since then. I'm not a slave to it, of course; yesterday I had a breakfast meeting at the time of that hour, so I moved the hour down. This morning I had to cut it to around 45 minutes, but did those 45 minutes diligently.

I started writing this novel just like I recommend starting a short story, by deciding what I needed and imagining the specifics of those people, places and events.

Now I have several pages of notes and am starting to get to that wonderful point when I'm thinking about the story spontaneously during the day and night, where my subconscious is starting to have fun with me and flicking out little bits of wonderful data about my people, their culture, what they look like and how they interact. Some of it is going in the direction I had planned, I do have a very specific theme for this book, but some of it is taking some delightful (and a bit delightfully dark) turns and entering in to areas of the psyche I hadn't realized would be involved.

Another thing I like to do is just get the ideas down, the thoughts, the imaginings, then look at them and see if they are hackneyed, cliché, un-thought-out, illogical, etc., then ask myself questions. "If this is true, how can this also be true?" or "Okay, that's been done so many times since the invention of myth that it looks like a Xerox copy. How can I turn that on its ear?"

I either answer the questions as soon as they're asked, even having a discussion with myself on paper about them, or let them ferment a bit. The answers to those questions, or the discussions I have with myself about them, are usually the very things that make the story rich for me, and, hopefully, will make it alive for a reader.

I love the delightful obsession, this passion, when it comes over me and I really love that I have the ability to engender it. And it becomes this passion simply because I treat it like a job.

When your writing is treated that way, you do it every day. When you treat it that way, you accomplish so much. You set a goal, you start and finish projects. You can move from "I am a writer" to "I'm a published writer."

14
Criticism and Praise

Enlightened Criticism

There is a point in the creation of art when you must encounter criticism. It is not to be avoided, in my opinion (although if you seek it out too soon, it can stop you from wanting to create.) In one of my many past incarnations, I was a theatre reviewer. I even had a site dedicated to small theatre in Los Angeles called LA Theatre Review. The discussion came up in an editorial meeting (there were five other writers who contributed to the site) about what a review actually is. My conviction is that a review, a critique of any piece of art, is a conversation.

As I have said many times, art is meant to be shared, and in being shared, it is meant to be discussed. The conversation between friends after going to a gallery or a theatre or movie house is, for me, almost as exciting as the actual gallery show, play or movie was. Those conversations are enlivening, energizing, inspirational. And often very, very funny. It fosters bonding on a very deep level.

So what is a review or critique? Consumer advocacy? A chance to sell tickets (or books, or canvases, etc.)? A description of the plot, or picture? Well, yes, I think a good review can include all of these things, but what I really think a review is is a conversation between the reviewer and the audience members who have seen or will possibly see the piece. Often, criticism in itself is an art. There are compilation of criticism that live longer than the original work of art, because the conversation is so intelligent, well thought out and entertaining. My mother used to subscribe to the New York Times Book Review insert. Not the whole paper, just that section. She read it cover to cover. Almost never bought the books discussed, but loved the discussion.

Analyzing a piece of work, expressing what effect it had on you, looking into the possibilities it opened up for you, inspired for you, is very a very exciting process to do for the critic and to read for the audience.

When it is time for you, when you encounter criticism of your writing, thinking of it as a conversation can be very powerful. You can learn from the conversation rather than be wounded by it. And you can contribute more to the conversation by continuing to write.

When We Fear Praise

Part of criticism is praise. I have often heard a variation of the comment that someone doesn't trust or can't accept praise. A good friend recently went as far as to say, "Don't tell me I'm special, I don't want to hear it."

There are many reasons to have this attitude:
- Not believing you could be special
- Thinking that whoever is praising you has some hidden or not so hidden agenda

- Believing it unseemly to tout one's own accomplishments
- Not wanting to "Raise One's Head Above the Crowd" for fear if it being lopped off
- Not wanting to get a big head
- Acute embarrassment at being singled out
- Acute embarrassment at it having taken so long to be singled out
- Not wanting to appear arrogant
- Really, really liking the praise and being fearful that, if you let people know that, they'll stop praising you.
- etc.

I have also been uncomfortable with praise. I'm sure for me it is a combination of any number of the above reasons, depending the day, the event and my circadian rhythm. Oddly, though, I have also always desperately sought praise. You'd think I'd be happy when I got it, but that would be too emotionally stable. The mental dissonance that praise often sets up can be very disconcerting and can itself cause the fear of it. The many separate thought waves that the praise sets in motion often momentarily overtake our ability to reason.

So. How do we strive for excellence if we fear praise? Praise is not a great reason to pursue excellence, but is a natural byproduct of it.

I have seen people who have a very gracious way of dealing with praise. They accept it. They don't add to it or try to diminish it or comment on it or make any judgments about the praise giver or try to appear humble in its presence, they simply accept it. What lovely and enviable equanimity. I've actually tried it. (Yes, I am publically admitting that I have received praise for my work.) When I simply accept it, whether I agree with the praise or not, whether I trust the praise giver or not, it immediately calms the dissonance in my

Poppycock!

head and allows me to actually enjoy my own accomplishments.
　That is only a good thing.

Part Three

The Nitty-Gritty

15
How to Rite Gud

What you will find in the final chapters of this book are exercises, thoughts, ideas and techniques that you can use when you are writing. They are mostly focused on writing fiction, but can be applied to any writing. Most can even be applied to other art forms entirely. We'll start with an easy one. Well, easy for someone who isn't Type A, anyway.

Daydream Yourself into Your Work

Much good writing, even fiction writing, requires research and study. If you want to get your story straight, as they say in the Cop shows, you need to know the facts that support and enhance your work. Even good fantasy has some root and basis in reality and science fiction will need a plausible scientific underpinning.

Sometimes, the "research" is just you making stuff up.

Either way, though, once you do the research, daydream. Think about the specific facts you've discovered (or created) in your research. Take these specific facts and make them real for yourself – imagine the size, shape, texture, smell, taste, color, sound of the things you've discovered. First, imagine them consciously; think about them, feel, see, taste, hear, smell them in your mind. Then, as they become more real, let them percolate into your subconscious. (Or, as Paul Sheele calls it, the "other than conscious" mind.)

Once you've let them go a little, sit and daydream. Daydream while you wash the dishes. Daydream while you do your laundry. Daydream in the shower and on the toilet. Don't daydream while you're driving (let's be logical about this daydreaming stuff,) but if you're sitting in the back seat, daydream! Sit on the couch and simply daydream.

When you daydream yourself into your work, you will be amazed at how easily the words flow once you finally sit down to map out your story. It's easy to tell a story that you've experienced in real life, and when you daydream about the circumstances of your story, you are experiencing it. In real life. Really. Your subconscious doesn't know the difference. To it, it's all just stuff to experience. The story will often "tell itself" after that.

This is what I think true inspiration is, you've done the work, now the Muse (your subconscious mind) feeds you the art.

Write What You See, Not What You Think You See

I took a drawing class once, not sure from whom, I was in high school at the time, where the teacher said, "Draw what you see, not what you think you see." After a moment to process this, my drawing improved unbelievably quickly. I was drawing a face at the time. I had put a nose where I knew noses were supposed to be, eyes in their proper place, a mouth down below. After that comment, I looked to see what was actually on the face I was drawing. It wasn't nose, eyes and mouth, it was specific shapes and shades of light and dark in specific relationships to each other. The drawing I produced was the best one I'd ever done to that point. Amazing what a simple adjustment in perspective will do.

There is a similar process in writing. People often write what they have been trained is there rather than what really is there. Rather than looking at the sky, they type blue. It's rarely just blue. Right now outside my window, it's a pale blue graduating toward dusky grey at the horizon. Rather than imagining the whole of something, people will parrot what they have heard others say. The cat doesn't just purr, she softly vibrates with pleasure, her eyes closed and her body relaxed, swaying back and forth gently to the slow rhythm of her breath.

Do you have to use all those words when you write? Do you have to describe every subtle detail? No. That would make your writing very tedious for you and for your reader. But when you really look at something, in your view or in your mind, you will know which of all those words to use that will most communicate it. Even if you end up just writing, "the cat purred", because you have first really looked, it will inform what comes before and what comes after and will make the word picture you're painting much more compelling.

Visceral Writing

I use the word "visceral" often to describe writing, or, at least, a certain kind of writing. What, exactly, do I mean by that word?

Webster's On-Line dictionary defines visceral thus:

vis cer al *adj.* \\'vi-sə-rəl, 'vis-rəl\\

1. felt in or as if in the viscera : deep "*a visceral conviction*"
2. not intellectual : instinctive, unreasoning "*visceral drives*"
3. dealing with crude or elemental emotions : earthy "*a visceral novel*"
4. of, relating to, or located on or among the viscera : splanchnic "*visceral organs*"

Viscera, used in the first and last definition means gut, so visceral writing is writing that is felt in the gut. Definition two implies that it is instinctive rather than intellectual, it isn't experienced by reason, so it isn't necessarily experienced in the head. Definition three talks about the more base or rude type of writing that might be found in Harlequin Romances and other soft-core porn, so, although I'm not opposed to that kind of communicating, it's not exactly what I mean.

What I mean when I use this word is writing that uses the senses, that uses experiences in the body to communicate a circumstance or idea.

Why is visceral writing more effective than intellectual or cerebral writing? This question assumes that the two are mutually exclusive, which I say isn't so. However, intellectual and cerebral writing can communicate much better if it also includes the visceral. The reason is that as human beings we first started experiencing the world through our senses, through the impressions we felt in our gut rather than the conclusions we made in our brain. As we grew older, many of us learned to trust the brain more than the gut, and many of us were encouraged in that by our teachers and mentors. However, even then, no matter how much we deny it, our feelings influence our mind.

Our language supports this: "We feel it in our gut" means we know it's right. When we are moved by a story, it "hits us in the gut".

Many studies that looked at how we decide things conclude that we make our decisions first in our gut or instinct, more immediately, and then we use our brains to understand or justify that derision. Why not bypass that understanding and justification and go straight for the gut?

Werner Erhartdt even went as far as to say that, "Understanding is the booby prize." Whatever you think of him, I agree with that. In Michael Novak's philosophical work, Ascent of the Mountain, Flight of the Dove, he talks about those who have had an experience (here he's talking about a religious or transcendent experience.) He posits that philosophy evolved to understand and explain such experiences, then grew to the point where these who studied them began to look down on those who actually experienced them. Then he argues passionately (that is a very visceral word) that the experience itself is much more powerful than the understanding of it.

I use the word visceral in regards to good writing because I believe feeling something is much more powerful than simply understanding it.

16
The Structure of Writing

Remember, there are no rules, only guidelines. That said, writing usually follows a structure, and the more you write, the more you read, the more that structure presents itself. Let's look at the three main parts of that structure: beginning, middle and end.

Beginnings at the Beginning

The western notion of story structure (no, it's not Universal) dictates a beginning, a middle and an end. It dictates setups and payoffs. It dictates some sort of change to happen to a circumstance or a character or both.

In the beginning, something happens that sets something else in motion. Pretty simple.

In linear story structure (1~2~3) the beginning happens where you would expect it, at the beginning, but there are many other ways of doing it. There is a device called framing, where you "frame" your story with the last scene.

(3~1~2~3.) Usually, with this device, the last scene is broken in two and the story starts with the first half and ends with the second half of that scene. Sometimes the last scene is repeated, but on the second reading, we know much more, so it seems new, the meanings of the moments seem different. The beginning happens second in this technique.

Sometime, you might tweak this even further and start at the middle, then go back to the beginning and tell the story through to the end. (2~1~2~3.) This can be a very exciting way to tell a story when handled well. It creates an immediate intrigue, then goes back to explain what lead up to it, how it happened, then resolves it.

One of my favorite nontraditional story telling techniques is the non-linear structure, where things happen completely out of sequence and the reader isn't sure of anything until the final moments of the story. (3~2~6~1~4. Or something.) In these, the beginning can be in the middle or, as with the movie "Memento", at the very end, or anywhere in between. This is a difficult device to use well, but when it is mastered, it can be thrilling to read because every moment keeps you guessing. A very formidable but gloriously satisfying (and marvelously surreal) novel that uses this technique is Samuel R. Delany's Dhalgren. That one not only starts somewhere in the middle, it starts mid-sentence!

Even within these nonlinear or nontraditional ways to tell a story, however, the piece itself has a beginning. It needs that moment or event that makes the reader want to know what's next. No matter where in your story you start, starting on something that creates tension or surprise or confusion or recognition or something is very highly recommended. At least in the Western notion of story structure.

Happy beginnings! The rest of the story is wide open!

The Muddle in the Middle

Now let's look at the middle.

Often, I've heard that the basic reason that much writing doesn't quite work is "the muddle in the middle." I think this can be true. A writer will have a great idea for a story, will know where it starts and know where it ends. He will write a great beginning, and a good or great ending. But then he must get from one to the other and is often confused as to how to do that.

First, remember that confusion is a very high and powerful state to be in. Don't fight it, celebrate it.

Then, there are things you can do to help you on your way.

What is the middle? What is set in motion in the beginning progresses and develops, often in unexpected ways. Again, pretty basic and simple.

The middle is also most of your story, not just the middle third of it. This intimidates some writers. Don't let it intimidate you. You're the one in charge of the beast and your story will thank you if you take the reins firmly. To stretch a metaphor a little. Which can be fun.

So what do you do? First, step away from the computer and do some imagining work. You'll need to know your characters. You'll need to know your settings. Imagine them well before you start to write. Give them quirks, if you want. The characters, I mean, not the settings. Although giving the settings quirks might be fun, too.

Once you've imagined them, write down what you imagined. This is for you, just notes, not part of the story itself, although much of it may end up in the story.

Once you've done this, if the getting from A to Z still doesn't become clear, throw some circumstances at your characters (or settings. Or both) to see how they would react to them. Again, this is just for yourself, but again, a lot of it could influence your story in very interesting ways.

The main piece of advice I have, however, once you feel you know your people and where and when they are sufficiently, is to imagine the unfolding of the events of the story. Live through it in the senses of your mind. Feel the events, smell them, hear them, see them, taste them. Do this before you are actually writing it all down. If something occurs to you in this imagining, make a note of it, but keep imagining.

Then just tell the tale you've imagined. This will be the basis of the story, and, since you've come to it organically and have personally experienced it yourself, anything that is missing will become obvious. The muddle will melt and the middle will move meaningfully forward. To use too many alliterations. Which can also be fun.

All's Well that Ends Well

Now I'll talk about endings, and use Mr. Shakespeare's title without compunction or permission.

What is an ending? That is where the ultimate consequence or result of what is set in motion in the middle is realized. (The ultimate consequence can be implied rather than explicitly described.) Again, simple.

Endings, however, in life and in stories, can be varied and can be confusing. They can be unsatisfying and they can be thought provoking. They can be trite, they can be abrupt, they can be sentimental. Some are happy, some tragic, some, contrived. Like in life, some are perfect, some are messy. Some stories, The Lady or the Tiger by Frank R. Stockton is a prime example, end by very consciously not ending. Don't be fooled. Even that influential story has an ending, it is just rather enigmatic.

Endings can also be circular, where they lead back to the beginning. They can actually be the beginning, as in Pinter's play Betrayal or Christopher Nolan's movie Memento. In both these examples, the beginning explains everything.

Often, stories will end at a new beginning. The hero will come home, look around at his life, then look out his door at the new possibilities and adventures awaiting him. (Hollywood loves this kind of ending, because it leaves the possibility of a lucrative sequel wide open.)

Many writers, notably O Henry and Guy de Maupassant, end their stories with a completely unexpected twist. This is a very satisfying, but not easy, technique. A twist that makes no sense is worse than a cliché ending. A twist has to make sense, given everything that has lead up to it. If you can master that, however, you will be a master story teller.

Some writers, especially beginning writers, will often be tempted to resolve every issue in the story, and resolve them completely. The cliché way to say this is "tie everything up with a neat bow". This is unnecessary. It is also rarely satisfying to the reader. Resolve your main conflicts if you must, but you can resolve them with a question rather than with an answer. This can leave the reader thinking.

Just because the ultimate consequence of what is set in motion are realized, it doesn't at all mean that it is all necessarily resolved.

I'll end this part about ending with a quote from novelist Jerry Pournelle. "And meanwhile, the storytellers like me and Anderson, Silverberg... we tell stories. People like them. They want to know how it comes out, they want to know what the ending is."

If your reader wants to know how things come out, in the end that's a good story. Even if you don't actually tell them.

17
Writing Fiction

Writing a Short Story

I love short stories. I have read them all my life. I have had subscriptions to New Yorker, AGNI, Omni, Asimov and other magazines just so I could read the short stories. I have collections from Esquire and the Saturday Evening Post. And, of course, many, many collections of science fiction short stories.

I have written short stories most of my life. I think I wrote my first one when I was, perhaps, eight or nine. My mother kept a copy of it, but I have no idea what has become of it. My earlier stories were dark and brooding, the product of a self-pitying teenaged mind. I still have a few of them around. They amuse me. I want to hug that kid, then tell him to get over it.

Over the years, I've honed my writing. Eventually, I began to notice that, although each story I wrote demanded its own creative process, I approached each one in a very similar way.

It seemed magical and intuitive, but there was something familiar about it each time.

Several years ago, about the same time I started writing with Steve Mancini, I started examining the process I used to write. It seemed very close, again, to the process Steve and I used to write together. I realized, as I looked at it dispassionately, that the process was repeatable, that it could be replicated. That it could be taught to others. This was an exciting discovery.

It seems to me that I've always heard that writing fiction seems a mystery to many who would love to do it. I am committed to people finding and pursuing their passions, and what better way than to de-mystify the process of writing a short story.

So I wrote a how-to guide on just that, called You Can Write a Short Story. Since I published it, I've have gotten several notes from people that, using the book and following along with it, they have written their first short story. Whenever I hear this, my chest glows a little with proud warmth. As I have said before, I cry at supermarket openings, so you know I tear up when we get those messages.

If you have ever thought you'd like to write, or if you've ever been confused by any of the parts of the process, I urge you to get that book. It's on Amazon.com If you are a writer and find yourself overwhelmed with ideas or lack any new ideas, or if you frequently experience what people call "writer's block", I urge you to get that book.

I won't go in to all the specifics again here, but I will give you some very powerful, general thoughts about writing short stories. (Or any fiction. Or even some non-fiction.)

Creating a Rich Environment

Where are you? Go ahead, look around. What do you see? What do you hear? What does the air feel like? Smell like?

What are you touching, and what's touching you? It feels real, doesn't it? It should because it's what we call reality.

Now, think of a place you've been – on vacation or in your neighborhood, anywhere you've been that you aren't at now. Imagine what you saw there. What did you hear? What did the air feel like? Smell like? What were you touching, what was touching you? Pretend you can actually see, hear, smell and feel those things in your body. Does it bring back more details as you imagine further? Does it feel real on any level? This is what we call memory.

Now think of a place you've never been. It can be on this planet or on a different one. It can be now or in the past or in the future, real, partly real or completely fictional. Now imagine what you might have seen there. What you would have heard. What the air would have felt like. Smelled like. Imagine what you would have been touching or what would have been touching you. Give each sense a moment. Give each sense more detail to play with. Can you get a visceral sense of the place? This is what we call imagination and is the basis for much good writing.

Whether you're writing fiction or reports, a letter or an article, if you need to create a rich environment to communicate something to your reader, the easiest way to do it is to first imagine it for yourself, imagine yourself in it. Even if it is an environment you are very familiar with, take a moment to let your body, your five senses, experience it. Take a moment to pretend you are there right now. Imagine moving around in that place.

Much of your writing will take care of itself at that point, and it will be filled with rich detail that more easily communicates to your reader.

Poppycock!

When Your Characters Speak to You

There are times when I don't get much writing done for an extended period of time. Is it writer's block? No. Absolutely not. Besides the fact that I have said many times I don't think there really is such a thing, my mind is usually swirling with ideas the whole time. Sometimes it's best to let them swirl (as long as you're not using that as another excuse not to get stuff done) until they coalesce into a form that's manageable.

I've talked about working on Old Magic. There was a time in the process when I didn't get much writing done on that. I'd done a ton of imagining work, though. So what are the ideas I'd been riding along, Dorothy-like, in the storm of my mind? Well, let me tell you. I suspected the novel would be dark, but in that period of apparent non-activity, one of the characters decided to have an affair with someone very inappropriate and two others informed me they are going to die quite unexpectedly, all in delightfully dark and twisted ways. I hadn't expected a lot of death in this novel, and now there will be at least two bodies. You will grieve for at least one of them.

Writers often talk about the point where the characters start telling you what they are doing, what they want, start moving in directions seemingly completely outside your plans for them. It's an exciting point to get to and I say 1) it is predictable and you can cause it to happen, and 2) they really aren't outside of you moving your pen at all. Both of these things are caused by what I have been saying all along about the process of writing:

If you imagine the circumstances of the people, places and events, using all five of your senses, and dream yourself through the story, you will be feeding your subconscious mind with information and with a command to be creative. Your subconscious loves this particular command and will bubble what you've fed to it, churn it, cook it and feed it back to you in ways that will surprise you. It will really seem as if the characters are talking to you, telling you that what you planned won't work, giving you suggestions or demands. Your subconscious has created these people to the point where it can't tell they are fiction. Your subconscious doesn't know what fiction is. To it, they really are real, perceived beings and circumstances and anything that don't make sense, the things you planned that aren't logical within the world you've created, won't be tolerated by the reality you have allowed your inner mind to grow and experience.

So even when I'm not actually writing, I can be being very productive. I can already hear Kyle's mother telling me to stop judging her.

Fictionalizing Stories from Life

If you are writing stories from your life, there are many reasons to fictionalize them, or at least fictionalize elements of them. I'm going to briefly focus on three:

- For your benefit
- For the benefit of the people you're writing about
- For the benefit of your reader

We'll start with the most obvious, for benefit of the people you're writing about.

The old cliché from the television show Dragnet that ran from 1951 through 1959, "... the names have been changed to protect the innocent." Often, though, just changing the name might be insufficient. Consider: You are writing a story about an experience that your child had. If you simply change his or her name, but leave the locations, characteristics and circumstances the same, it will become very obvious to anyone who cares to look who the model was. The child will grow up and feel violated by the story. I rather doubt that a parent would want to make their child feel violated.

In this case, I recommend changing enough that the essence of the story is still there, but the particulars are imagined as if the entire thing were a fictional story you're writing. If your child is named Bill, consider changing it to Janice. This will immediately remove the story from specifics that will embarrass the child.

If the person isn't a child, some of the same things might apply.

For Your Readers

When you write something from your life, you are crammed with information about the incident or incidents. There are things that happened in real life at the same time that aren't really directly related to the incident. There are steps that happened that are really inconsequential to it. It is very difficult to edit these things out because it feels like a violation of the truth and you are telling the story, after all, because it is the truth. (I realize the irony, but I say that by fictionalizing it, you are telling a bigger truth.)

By giving yourself fictional elements, you must then really look at what the point of the story is, what beginning, middle and end that would express that point and what people you need for that. It becomes much easier to edit a story that you aren't as invested in. In reality, the third and fourth time your teacher screamed at you were as awful to experience as the first. For a reader, however, the first and second will probably be more than sufficient to get the point across and more than that might make their mind wander. (Don't look at the numbers, here, look at the point itself. I know you wouldn't be all rigorous on my math, but I must say that for my own sake.)

Here is where fictionalizing can be powerful for the reader.

For Yourself

The parody of the Dragnet quote is, "The names have been changed to protect the guilty." This was funny through about the mid-sixties, but it is important, here. Besides the benefit for you of making it easier to edit, fictionalizing your story will make it much less likely that you will be sued, or, at the very least, harassed by someone you have exposed or profiled.

This is not a small thing.

As I said, this is a brief discussion of why fictionalizing a story from your life might be effective or wise. These are not rules. (You may have noticed that I don't much like rules when it comes to creativity.) So forget everything I just said and go write your life.

Darkness Falls

You are a light and optimistic person. You decide to write something. When you are finished, you are horrified to discover you've written a dark, brooding, perhaps even violent piece. Where did that come from? After all, you are light. You are optimistic. Perhaps this writing thing is just too dangerous.

Poppycock. We all have aspects of ourselves that look toward the dark side of life. Even the most angelic among us, and there are angels among us, have a corner of their psyche that doesn't reflect the glow of love and gentle kindness. To be truly enlightened, one must acknowledge these corners, embrace them as part of what makes the perfect whole of ourselves. If not expressed, these corners fester and can overwhelm us.

What better place to acknowledge them, than, but in art? It is personal enough to get the truth into the light of day and impersonal enough to be able to be called fiction. Far from dangerous, it is actually a very safe outlet. I am one of the most optimistic, peaceful people I know and yet I have written often of death, murder and torture. I used to be surprised when I did. Now I just accept it as something that needs expression.

And why would a reader want to read such a piece? As with the writer, to shine the light on those same corners within themselves. And it can be thrilling, titillating, to read.

If you sit down to write and darkness falls on your paper, celebrate it as much as you would an ode to beauty. It is a wonderful expression of part of beautiful you.

18
Some Writer's Exercises

Over the years, I have developed several exercises for the writer. Most can be used in to enhance any art. I recommend trying one or two:

A Writer's "Finger Exercise"

When a music student learns to play the piano (or the horn, I imagine) his teacher will give him finger exercises do daily to condition his fingers and his ears to become limber, to know where the notes are, to know how to move from one to another and know what they sound like. The music student who becomes proficient continues doing these exercises to keep the skills and awareness they developed sharp.

A writer's tools are his five senses: Sight, sound, smell, taste and touch. When I was an acting teacher for all those years, all those years ago, I developed a series of "Actors' Finger Exercises" in order to have my students become more aware of and tuned in to how to use their own tools. I will now provide these exercises here for the writer. They apply with very little adjustment:

- At the beginning of the week, every week, chose one of the senses. (We'll start with "Smell" in order to illustrate.)
- As you go about your day, stop and notice that one sense (smell) for a moment. "This week I'm noticing smell. What do I smell right now?"
- Just notice. Don't try to interpret, don't try to make it mean anything. Just notice what smell or smells are there in your immediate environment.
- Think briefly of the qualities of those particular odors.
- Do this a couple of times a day. It only takes a second or two.
- At the end of the week (you can do this every day, if you'd like) write down short descriptions of several of the smells you encountered during your week, and try to imagine you are smelling them as you write.

The next week, choose another sense, say "Touch" and do the same thing with that. As you go about your day, stop and touch something, a tree or a bench, or the pants you're wearing. At the end of the week, write down short descriptions of several of the textures and surfaces you touched. Try to re-experience them as you write.

Repeat with sight, then sound, then taste.

Then repeat the cycle again, several times for several weeks. Some of my acting students did these exercises every week for several years because they got so much benefit from them.

What are some of the benefit you can expect?

- You will become more aware of your senses

- You will train your body and mind to be able to recreate the sensations
- You will train your mind to notice subtle things, under and behind the obvious
- Because you can re-experience them, you will have greater ability to express them to your reader
- Your writing will become richer
- When you are creating a fully fantastical environment, you can incorporate new and exciting sights, sounds, smells, tastes and textures because you will be able to imagine them and experience them and communicate that experience to your reader

Visceral writing, especially but not only in fiction, pulls the reader in.

Observing

All artists have exercises to help them with the craft of their art. Painters and sculptors are always sketching. Musicians do scales and are always plinking and plunking and tinkling on something. Dancers do their bar work. Singers do vocal warmups.

An exercise I recommend for writers is to sit down, look at something in your immediate environment or out the window and write down what you see. Write it in detail that you would never include in a story. Use as many of your senses as you can. It is a very good way to flex your observation muscles and your facility with words, with evoking an experience. And you never know, you may end up using a lot of them in some form in your writing.

When I was taking care of my mother in her cabin in Northern Idaho, everything was new and different for me. I didn't have much to do most of the day, so I started describing the things in her living room, the hummingbirds drinking out of the red, red feeder right outside the window, the way the shadows of the clouds rolled over the green fields of the valley beyond. I described the yellow flowers on the hill behind the cabin. I described a wonderful thunder and lightning storm that I watched travel toward us from a long way off one bright night.

These exercises, done over weeks, became an integral part of one of the plots of my novel Guardian Mosaic.

When I got back home, I was still in the habit of observing and writing what I saw in my immediate surroundings. I described my own tiny living room with new eyes, having not seen it for several months. This became part of what I consider to be the best thing I've ever written, a surreal prose poem about my mother's death called A Journey Home.

Even if you never use the actual descriptions, it's a wonderful, rich thing to do. And you'll never know if there's something there to eventually use if you don't try!

There is Always Something to Write

When you find you have nothing to write, or think you have nothing to write, focus in on some one sense. For today, simply let the feel of the air suggest something. First experience it. What exactly does it feel like? Then let your imagination wander. What does it suggest? Again, with all writing exercises, you may or may not use this in any actual piece, but the act of writing begets the act of writing. The act of imagining begets the act of imagining. And if you let it, you will find something beautiful on your page that you may just want to use, as is or adjusted, in your next story.

I call this exercise "Observe, then Imagine".

Here is mine:

There is a chill in the air in Los Angeles that reminds me pleasantly of autumns from my childhood. The trees are rustling provocatively, as if they are anticipating something big and want to be prepared for it. The rustling comes in waves, each with its own small crescendo, and, like waves in a restless sea, some are stronger, more sustained than others, and the stillness between them more filled with that anticipation.

I imagine a fireplace waiting for me somewhere, perhaps a dog lying on a rug by the door with his head on his paws. He is old enough to be settled, but young enough to sill want to play on occasion, big and friendly and just seeing him makes you want to thump his side. I imagine an old, comfortable couch with an old, hand-made afghan thrown haphazardly over the back, ready to be pulled around my shoulders as I settle in with a leather-bound book, the dog curling up beside me to nap as I read.

I imagine the smells of winter cooking riding out of a kitchen on heavy air, thick with moisture from the boiling sauces. (Actually, it's not hard at all to imagine that; there is a nice, thick red sauce simmering in the other room, lush with bobbing, home-made meatballs.)

I imagine the house is in a clearing in the woods, made of stone and wood, and the rustling trees outside foretell a winter storm that will overnight cover the house and grounds in a deep, white coat of snow that will insulate me from the rest of the world and will necessitate building a blazing fire in the fireplace.

I imagine that fire, the pungent, comforting and comfortable spicy smell of burning oak, the noise the air makes as it rushes up the chimney, layered with arrhythmic crackles and pops.

What did you feel? And what did that suggest for you?

Stream-of-Consciousness Exercise

I have talked often about the stream-of-consciousness exercise and how powerful it is for any writer or creative person. I first encountered a version of it from reading Julia Cameron's The Artist's Way. She called it "The Morning Pages" and hers is a little different from mine, but either will do.

The idea of this exercise is to open up the communication between you and your subconscious mind. It is a way for the subconscious to feed you some of the lovely things it has been cooking up as it churns all the data you have given it. It is also a way to keep your conscious mind engaged so it won't get in your way, which is something it dearly loves to do.

I recommend you do this exercise every day for three to five minutes. Yes, I said every day. You can spare three to five minutes if it will enhance your creativity, which, of course, will enhance your life.

The exercise is very simple. It is best if you do it long-hand because that is a more visceral experience, but if you must, type it in a document on your computer. (I actually have to do it on the computer because my hand cramps up when I write long-hand, so there you are.)

It's kind of like journaling, but not in the "I saw a kitty today on my walk" sense. Sit down with your pad and pen, or at your keyboard, and simply write out what is in your mind. As you write, don't be creative. Don't be brilliant. Don't edit what you're writing. Be boring. Be sloppy. Don't direct your mind, only write what's there. Even if what's there is "I hate Geoff. This exercise is stupid. I really hate this. Nothing is happening. I hate this."

As you write or type, don't stop to think. Just keep going. Don't go over it, either. If you do this every day for several days, I guarantee you that you will start to notice some very odd and interesting ideas appear on the page as if by magic. For many it will start happening on the second or third day. If you are a particularly stubborn case, it could take as much as four or five days, but ideas will appear.

As I say, don't go back and read what you've written right away. After a day or so, you can go back and see what's there. Some of it will surprise you. You will have no memory of having written it at all. I did this exercise every morning for several years. I don't much, anymore, since I have a fairly fluid communication with my subconscious mind, but do go back to it when I start to feel unconnected.

As you do this, ideas will not only appear on your page (I once got an idea for a very cool short story from something that I found in my pages) but it will also generally open up the communication with the subconscious mind and you will notice that ideas begin to show up for you throughout your day.

Try it. I guarantee it will work!

Use Everything as an Excuse to Write

It is very close to Thanksgiving in the United States of America, a time when some minds turn towards gluttonous indulgences. Don't get me wrong, I am grateful for gluttonous indulgences. I am also grateful for living somewhere where I can indulge in them.

Before this gets entirely too maudlin and trite, let me say that, for a writer, everything is an excuse to write, giving thanks doubly so. What are you grateful for? What do you most appreciate in your life? I am firmly convinced that, if we were all to spend five minutes every morning reminding ourselves of what we had to be grateful for, our lives would transform. Couple that with spending five to ten minutes writing stream of consciousness and you have the possibility of creating the true life of a writer.

So, what am I grateful for? The list is very long, but I'll try to do it justice.

Los Angeles – I have the privilege of living in a city whose very reason to be is creativity.

My poor old cat – she is annoying and senile and I do love her very much. Her name is Cat.

My days – I work 12 to 15 hours every day, but I do that for myself and there's no greater bounty.

My writing partner Steve – I have said it often, but what we create together is miraculous, mercurial and unpredictable and far beyond what either of us could do on our own.

My family – My brothers and sister, David, Liam and Rachel, and their children and (gasp) grandchildren, my father's second family, Carol, Ann, Paul and Natalie and their children and (double gasp) grandchildren – I have somehow been attached to an extended family with more talent, love and creativity than most whole cities possess. I must have done something nice in a past life.

Computers – without them, I probably would be a very different person living a very different life.

Movies – the lights dim, the ads and previews run and my heart starts to beat faster. Then it goes black and the first sound or image assaults or massages me and I willingly leave this existence and enter a completely new one with infinite possibilities.

Friends – If I named any I would feel bad for not naming them all.

Mentors – I have to list two that have been and are very powerful forces in my life, Pat O'Bryan and Connie Ragen Green. They have both shown me more of what I was capable than I knew.

My little apartment and my landlord – It is warm and safe here and I'm surrounded by people who look after each other.

Imagination – who and where would I be without it? I can't imagine.

Good food and drink – being able to put fresh garlic, sage, salt, pepper and a touch of oregano into a mortar and grind them all with a pestle, add olive oil and a touch of vinegar, coat a pork roast with the mixture and bake until it's become a crust, then take the pan juices, add corn starch and make a gravy, is part of what makes life worth living. Well, eating the resulting feast is pretty good, too.

Books – Like movies, but they last longer and I go deeper.

Being a best-selling author.

Being a teacher – here, it is appropriate to mention that what I am most grateful for is the trust and faith that the people who choose to learn from me provide, and how much I learn and grow from their questions, understanding, disagreements and growth.

Silliness – without that I wouldn't be a best-selling author.

There is more. I am grateful that you read this. I would be grateful if you shared some of what you see around you.

Be a Tree

There is an exercise that is often taught in acting classes, and most actors hate it. They not only hate it, they deride it and spend countless years after their initial training parodying it and using it as an example of why it's completely useless to study acting. That exercise is to "Be a Tree."

It's an exercise that I actually like, although I teach it slightly differently, I think, than some do.

- Stand or sit. Standing is probably better, but it isn't really important.
- Shut your eyes or keep them open. Actually, keeping them open might work better for

various reasons, but again, it isn't really important.
- Feel your roots. Here's where it gets squidgy for some actors. "I don't have any roots," they think. Feel them anyway. Feel them spreading out into the ground beneath you. Feel them pulling water and nutrients from the soil. Feel the moisture moving up them into your trunk.
- Feel your trunk. Same as above. It doesn't matter if you don't have one. Feel the rough bark on your surface, the more spongy interior that is pulling the water from your roots and sending it up to your branches and leaves, that is taking the energy from your leaves down to your roots so they can grow further out into the soil.
- Feel your branches and leaves. Feel the warm sunlight shining on your leaves and the energy you pull from it and send down your trunk to your roots.
- Feel the breeze moving your leaves, your branches. The gentle sway it causes.
- Notice the squirrel running up your trunk and down your branches. Notice the family of birds there. Hear the chicks begging the parents for food.
- Stay with this for a while.

Why do I like this exercise? Besides that I'm odd and think it's fun (I once pretended to be a salmon swimming upstream to spawn), it also opens up your ability to imagine, to experience that which is, by definition, foreign to you. As a writer, you will often require of yourself that you develop and make real something you haven't and couldn't experience. Your ability to imagine it fully and viscerally is vital. The more you practice this, the easier it is when you need it.

So, be a tree.

19
And So It Goes

I've been writing this book on and off for years. Did I know I would complete the challenge when I started it? No, of course not. I was determined to finish it, but didn't know whether or not I could, didn't know if I'd have that much to say. What I decided to do, then, was just do what I normally do, write about the process of writing. It's something I know a lot about, have done a fair amount of study on and have done the practical bit of actually writing.

Because of the commitment to write the book and the commitment to have it be worthwhile and useful, ideas seemed to come to me about subjects I could write about. There were days, however, when the idea wasn't right there, but my thought was, what if I were Dave Berry or Erma Bombeck and had to write an article every week day of my entire life? Not having an idea isn't an excuse when you're getting paid buckets of money. So how do you find something worthwhile to write about?

I talk about this in terms of fiction a lot. When you're stuck, journal in a stream-of-consciousness way. Just write. Write anything. (Or type anything.) Even if it's "I don't have any idea what to write. I still don't have any idea what to write. No ideas are coming to me in this stupid exercise." Even that will work. Also, I recommend imagining work. Imagine yourself into other circumstances and lives using your five senses.

I also suggest to look around yourself and simply described something or someone you can see. The lamp. The cat. Your brother-in-law. Again, use all five senses.

Do these ideas work for non-fiction, for writing informational articles or creating information products? As they say in Sweden, Ya, sure, you betcha. For some of the chapters I wrote for this book, I looked at questions that people asked me about writing. I also looked at questions I've always asked, some of which I hadn't yet found answers to. I imagined myself as a new writer, to remember what it felt like to not know anything about it. I looked around my living room and allowed things to make suggestions to me.

And sometimes, I just started typing. You'd think that most of what I typed when I did that wouldn't end up in the final draft, but you'd be surprised at how much would. I know I was surprised, even though I've used that technique often in my writing career. I would just start typing nonsense, and sense would show up quite uninvited. All by itself. Ideas would appear. The subconscious has lots to give back to us because we've fed it so much information. And it doesn't like to stay quiet, so when you just type randomly, the subconscious will have its way.

Then it was just a matter of shaping those ideas, expanding on them, doing any research necessary and allowing them to be written.

I trust that you have found something useful in the book. I trust that your thoughts have been provoked, and your creativity intrigued. I know you've probably disagreed with some of it, and to that I say, Very Good! If everyone agreed with everything, the world would be a very boring place, and none of us would have much opportunity to learn and grow.

To finish the book, then, I say again, continue writing! It's what a writer does.

Resources

Here are some resources that I have mentioned in the book, or that you may find useful:

The link to the review of *Weeping Willow: Welcome to River Bend* by Writer's Digest:
http://josephcoaler.com/testimonials.html#digest

Some of my books (and a free short story) can be found here:
http://StoriesByGeoff.com

My main site:
http://GeoffHoff.com

My writing blog:
http://tipsonwriting.net/blog/

My personal (humor and rant) blog:
http://ThatWouldBeMe.net

A short story writing course:
http://writingashortstory.com/

A book writing course:
http://YouCanWriteABook.net

About the Author

GEOFF HOFF is a best-selling author of fiction, business and how-to books. He has worn many costumes throughout his life. He was once "the good guy". He spent some time experimenting with "make everyone feel comfortable". Lately, he has discovered his inner curmudgeon and rather likes the outfit. The logical next garb to don is "old foggy" and he looks forward to that with great anticipation.

Geoff started writing fiction when he was a child, started acting in high school, sang with his family most of his life and has spent the last forty years studying the process of creativity.

Geoff grew up in a small town in Northern New Jersey that no longer exists, graduated from a small college in Spokane, Washington that no longer exists and has learned to distrust permanence.

You can find him at http://GeoffHoff.com When you visit his site, be sure to pick up his free report on what inspiration really is and how you can harness it for yourself and your business.

www.ingramcontent.com/pod-product-compliance
Lightning Source LLC
Chambersburg PA
CBHW070642050426
42451CB00008B/268